Metadata for Digital Resources

CHANDOS
INFORMATION PROFESSIONAL SERIES

Series Editor: Ruth Rikowski
(email: Rikowskigr@aol.com)

Chandos' new series of books are aimed at the busy information professional. They have been specially commissioned to provide the reader with an authoritative view of current thinking. They are designed to provide easy-to-read and (most importantly) practical coverage of topics that are of interest to librarians and other information professionals. If you would like a full listing of current and forthcoming titles, please visit our web site **www.chandospublishing.com** or contact Hannah Grace-Williams on email info@chandospublishing.com or telephone number +44 (0) 1993 848726.

New authors: we are always pleased to receive ideas for new titles; if you would like to write a book for Chandos, please contact Dr Glyn Jones on email gjones@chandospublishing.com or telephone number +44 (0) 1993 848726.

Bulk orders: some organisations buy a number of copies of our books. If you are interested in doing this, we would be pleased to discuss a discount. Please contact Hannah Grace-Williams on email info@chandospublishing.com or telephone number +44 (0) 1993 848726.

Metadata for Digital Resources

Implementation, Systems Design and Interoperability

MURIEL FOULONNEAU
AND
JENN RILEY

Chandos Publishing
Oxford · England

Chandos Publishing (Oxford) Limited
TBAC Business Centre
Avenue 4
Station Lane
Witney
Oxford OX28 4BN
UK
Tel: +44 (0) 1993 848726 Fax: +44 (0) 1865 884448
Email: info@chandospublishing.com
www.chandospublishing.com

First published in Great Britain in 2008

ISBN:
978 1 84334 301 1 (paperback)
978 1 84334 302 8 (hardback)
1 84334 301 0 (paperback)
1 84334 302 9 (hardback)

© M. Foulonneau, J. Riley, 2008

Typeset by Domex e-Data Pvt. Ltd.
Printed in the UK and USA.

Contents

List of figures, table and boxes

Figures

Table

Boxes

Acknowledgements

The authors would like to thank the Indiana University Libraries, the talented staff of the Indiana University Digital Library Program, and the Digital Library Research Laboratory and the group of researchers, students and practitioners that attend the metadata roundtable at the University of Illinois at Urbana-Champaign for the support they have provided for the authors' research. The authors have also greatly benefited from the work carried out by the Digital Library Federation and National Science Digital Library working group on *Best Practices for OAI Data Provider Implementations and Shareable Metadata* and in particular Sarah L. Shreeves and Kat Hagedorn, who led those discussions. Finally, the authors would like to thank Jean-Pierre Dalbéra, who has initiated applications in Europe to provide a single access point to resources from different cultural heritage sectors.

About the authors

Muriel Foulonneau was project coordinator at the University of Illinois at Urbana-Champaign for the CIC-OAI metadata harvesting project (2004–2006), an initiative for developing common best practices for sharing metadata among the Commitee for Institutional Cooperation consortium of research universities in the USA. She was part of the American initiative to create the Digital Library Federation and National Science Digital Library's *Best Practices for OAI Data Provider Implementations and Shareable Metadata,* and previously worked as a consultant in content management systems and as an IT advisor for the French Ministry of Culture. Muriel was a participant in the Minerva project, a collaboration among European ministries of culture on digitisation of cultural heritage resources (from libraries, museums, archives, archaeological sites, and so on). She also served as an expert for the European Commission for research projects related to digital heritage and research infrastructures. Muriel is the co-chair of the Dublin Core Collection Working Group of the Dublin Core Metadata Initiative. Since September 2006, Muriel has worked at the Centre pour la Communication Scientifique Directe of the CNRS in France where she works on the HAL archive of scientific publications and the European project DRIVER (Digital Repository Infrastructure Vision for European Research). Muriel is the author of numerous articles on digital libraries and metadata, and is the co-author of a book on the *Open Archives Initiative Protocol for Metadata Harvesting.*

Jenn Riley is the Metadata Librarian with the Digital Library Program at Indiana University, Bloomington, where she is responsible for planning metadata strategy for digital library projects and participates in the collaborative design of digital library systems. Much of her recent efforts have been working towards the cost-effective creation of 'shareable' metadata, promoting re-use of descriptive metadata in new and unanticipated environments. She was a major contributor to the emerging metadata guidelines *Best Practices for OAI Data Provider*

Implementations and Shareable Metadata from the Digital Library Federation and National Science Digital Library, and the *Digital Library Federation/Aquifer Implementation Guidelines for Shareable MODS Records.* Jenn's research interests also include the incorporation of thesaurus structures into search and browse systems, music digital libraries, and FRBR. Jenn is the author of the blog *Inquiring Librarian*, where her posts frequently centre around improving intellectual access to library materials, a contributor to the collaborative Blog and Wiki *TechEssence*, a technology resource for library administrators, and the author or co-author of a number of articles describing various aspects of developing digital library collections. In addition to an MLS from Indiana University, she holds a BM in Music Education from the University of Miami (Florida) and an MA in Musicology from Indiana University.

Part I
Introduction

What is metadata?

Metadata is often defined as 'data about data'.[1] That basic definition isn't very informative, however. Priscilla Caplan follows her introduction of the short definition of the term with a much more useful one: '*Metadata* is here used to mean structured information about an information resource of any media type or format'.[2] The notion of *structured* information is an important one; metadata in the cultural heritage sector tends to be highly structured. Others take a more philosophical approach to the definition of metadata, for example, the <indecs> metadata framework describes it this way: 'An item of metadata is a relationship that someone claims to exist between two entities'.[3] Still others, such as Lorcan Dempsey, focus instead on what metadata can *do*: 'I like to think of metadata as data which removes from a user (human or machine) the need to have full advance knowledge of the existence or characteristics of things of potential interest in the environment'.[4] Both of these latter two definitions acknowledge the role of a particular environment or set of expectations in defining what is considered metadata – information of interest to one community may be irrelevant to another.

The explanations and advice given in this book focus on metadata that's useful for the 'cultural heritage' sector: libraries, museums, archives, historical societies, and so on. These institutions are sometimes called 'memory' institutions. Although the word 'cultural' implies to some a focus on the arts and humanities, cultural heritage institutions as described here are concerned with the output of humans in all areas, including the hard sciences and social sciences in addition to arts and humanities. The approach to metadata in this book keeps with the overall mission of cultural heritage institutions: to collect (including virtually!), describe, and preserve the products of human endeavour in a wide variety of areas.

The term metadata, as used in this book, includes a variety of information that allows a user (which could be either a human or machine) to interact with objects. Metadata has aptly been compared to labels on cans in the supermarket.[5] Without labels, we would have to open all the cans to see what is in them, we would have to analyse their contents to know whether the substance is edible or not, and so on. Thanks to the labels, we know what the food is, what it is made of, where it comes from, how much it costs, up to what date we can safely eat it, possibly how we can prepare it and how to preserve it. In the cultural heritage sector, metadata can include the title of a journal article, the date it was written or published, the character encoding used in a particular version on the Web, the name of its rights holders, and the like.

The increasing importance of metadata

While some definitions of metadata restrict it to those aspects that apply to digital resources, the approach taken in this book is that metadata can describe physical (analogue) resources as well. The cultural heritage sector has a long history of using metadata to organise, manage, describe or retrieve resources in many forms, including catalogues, inventories and registers, long before digital resources existed. The role of metadata within cultural heritage institutions has increased over time, in terms of the functions it provides and the user interactions it enables, as institutional missions have expanded along with the types of material collected. Material that these institutions curate, archive, display and organise is increasingly digital. Competencies of staff and institutional policies are evolving to match the shifts in collection focus. Digital resources are stored on computers, not on stacks or in boxes, and therefore the types of problems that arise for the long-term preservation of these materials are less about moisture or insects and more about technological change and the life cycle of digital media.

Resources that were digitised from physical originals need metadata to trace their creation process to support an institution's management function, in addition to descriptive information about the original object. Digital resources, however, are not only digital versions of pre-existing analogue materials, but also can be online videos, games, software, datasets, scholarly articles written in a word processor, pictures taken with a digital camera, and so on. Some digital resources come from commercial sources and might contain digital rights management features enforcing certain use restrictions. Digital resources are increasingly being distributed widely and become divorced from their original context. Notions of peer review and the definition of 'quality' are evolving, with libraries, for instance, handling more and more material that is self-archived in institutional repositories and selecting material for preservation that is self-published over the Web.[6] All of these elements of change are affecting how cultural heritage institutions accomplish their mission, and metadata is a key element in evolving workflows.

In a digital environment, it is orders of magnitude easier to copy, modify and exchange content. The concepts of versions and information traceability have become extremely important because of the fluid nature of digital objects. This fluidity raises new challenges, but also allows new types of services to be built on top of digital resources.

Metadata creators

Many different individuals can participate in the act of metadata creation: a catalogue librarian can create a structured description for a published book; a museum curator can provide the appropriate historical context for a digital image of an object; an individual can create metadata for his personal web pages and the resources they contain – and the application with which he creates the web pages may have created additional metadata to specify the name of the application, the encoding it used, etc. A web-based application can allow end-users to tag a resource with terminology meaningful to that user. Specialists in a given knowledge domain can be invited to add information about a resource to a shared system. The perspective of each of those agents is necessarily different – each envisions a specific set of functions that a digital library system should support.

Much metadata is subjective in nature – What is important about this resource to record? What is this book about? To which other artists does this painting owe its inspiration? – so two highly-qualified individuals can have differing interpretations of the same object, both of them perfectly reasonable. Potentially contradictory data about an object may exist, posing challenges to the usability of that metadata. This potential disagreement, uncertainty, and inconsistency highlight the need for careful planning of the metadata creation process. But it also presents an opportunity to confront different perspectives on a resource.

This diversity of metadata creators and the ease with which new usage models can appear, leading to a need for re-purposing existing metadata, is an area of considerable change facing the cultural heritage sector at this time. The flexibility and modularity of metadata is a key component of the evolution of online services.

Metadata in digital library applications

As defined above, metadata is structured information about a digital resource and its properties. Metadata allows various functions to be performed on digital resources, for example, discovery, interpretation, preservation, management, representation and re-use of objects. A group of metadata elements developed for a defined purpose is commonly referred to as a *metadata format* or a *metadata structure standard*. As described in greater depth in Chapter 2, metadata formats are usually classified as *descriptive*, *administrative* or *structural*.[7] Preservation and rights metadata are generally included within the administrative metadata category. This classification, however, is rarely perfect; most metadata formats contain elements for more than one of these purposes.

A metadata format includes a list of metadata elements – often referred to as a data dictionary – with definitions and perhaps some guidance on how the elements should be populated. Again, a metadata format is generally developed with a specific purpose in mind. The Dublin Core Metadata Element Set, for example, was originally envisioned as a minimal element set for enabling resource discovery in a Web environment.[8] Metadata formats can be expressed in the form of a text that specifies for a human reader the set of rules attached to the object. In this case, a metadata creator only has to refer to the text in order to ensure compliance. A metadata format can also be expressed in a machine-readable format, for instance as an XML[9] or SGML[10] DTD, as an XML Schema, or as a RDF[11] schema. In those cases, the set of rules that define the metadata format can be validated by an application. The application reads the metadata record as well as the DTD or schema to verify the compliance of the record. A metadata format might also be expressed in multiple languages: for example, the simple Dublin Core format is expressed as text on the Dublin Core website as an XML Schema and as an RDF schema.

Metadata creation has a cost, both when it is created automatically and when it is created by humans, and that cost grows as the level of human intervention grows. In particular, metadata that requires interpretation of a resource or contextual knowledge in a given domain is difficult to extract from a resource itself. Therefore metadata is usually created with specific applications in mind. All types of metadata are not necessarily created together, by the same process, for the same application.

If a set of digital resources are described in the same metadata format according to similar rules, then an application can use this metadata to provide services more easily. The application can rely on the fact, for example, that a date property will be available for a given resource and that it will contain a date of creation of the resource in a given format, e.g., YYYY-MM-DD. With this level of consistency, it will be possible for the application to include the resource in, for example, a *sort by date* function or a graphic representation of a chronology.

To provide a user with a service, an application may not need to handle a resource itself but only a representation of the resource in the form of a metadata record. The application can rely on the information stored in metadata elements in order to identify a property of a resource, for example, the author of a peer-reviewed journal article. As applications and user needs have changed over time, new applications have used existing metadata formats to enable new interactions with digital objects. Often, this re-purposing of data requires moving data from one format to another. The act of transforming a metadata record in a given format into another record in another format is called crosswalking or mapping.

Location of metadata

A digital resource can be documented by one or more metadata records. A metadata record is an instance of a metadata element set, complying with a given metadata format. It contains values for elements describing properties for that specific object. A metadata record can be stored at the same place as the object (inside the object), outside the object and linked to it, or even handled by a third party. A TEI document,[12] for example, or an HTML web page, contains both a header with descriptive metadata and the text of a document itself. Certain file formats that allow embedded metadata, such as SVG,[13] require specialised applications to render the object and its metadata.

A library catalogue, by contrast, stores metadata records but not the digital objects themselves. Cultural heritage institutions are increasingly using digital content management systems, such as CONTENTdm,[14] to store both digital objects and metadata records in the same application. In this case, the metadata record is still generally stored either in a database or as a separate file, both distinct from the digital resource.

In still other cases, metadata records may be handled by a third party. This is the case in many applications based on the Open Archives Initiative Protocol for Metadata Harvesting (see Chapter 10) and general Web search engines. A third party website might display titles and creators of digital resources, or perform a search across records from a variety of institutions. But this third party site will likely only host the metadata records. If a user wants to access the digital object, he must follow a link to obtain the resource from the home institution.

Thinking widely about metadata

As illustrated above, metadata include many types of information created by a variety of actors. Metadata is not limited to the rule-based, structured data of the sort found in library catalogues. Metadata can appear under different labels in a variety of types, formats, and origins.

Tagging is a form of metadata made popular via social networking websites. Here, a tag is simply a term or string associated with an object. The exact relationship between the tag and the object is generally unspecified (although experiments with 'semantic' tagging are becoming more common), with the tag fulfilling a keyword-like role. A tag does not have to be part of an element set; instead, it represents a potentially more fuzzy and modular conception of metadata. It is likely that the dividing line between tagging and more structured forms of metadata creation will become less firm over time.

Annotations are data associated with a digital object or one of its parts, representing metadata added to a resource after its initial creation. In the context of the Internet, annotations can be added to a digital object and shared with a larger community. An important characteristic of annotations is that they represent explicitly what a viewer thought of or wanted to add with his or her own perspective to the digital object. Annotations can be in many forms, but usually are more than just a keyword. They can be written in natural language, and applied to a specific component of a digital object. Annotations are generally created to allow future interpretation of part or all of a resource, rather than being used for retrieval. The usage of the term is however still evolving and is sometimes used as a synonym for metadata in social applications. In both cases, however, it emphasises the role of metadata as subjective perspectives on a digital resource.

Document markup, or, more specifically, text encoding, is another form of metadata that falls outside the traditional notion of description in cultural heritage institutions. This process consists of specifying the formatting as well as the semantic structure of a document. Features such as headings, place names, and line breaks can all be marked within the document. The markup indicating these features is metadata, but of a different sort. Just like annotations, markup can interpret a part of a resource. Specific tags such as notes can be used to add information about a part of the text, and can be considered annotations or metadata about those parts. Encoding standards such as TEI also include metadata that supports the tracking of information added to the text over time.

The types of metadata described here address needs of different users and of different types of applications. They also enable interactions with the digital resources. This diversity of uses demonstrates that a traditional conception of metadata as a pre-conceived set of information that will enable a pre-conceived set of functions on the object can be adapted to a more modular structure, with more potential for re-usability in new and different applications. Generally, all but the most basic access requires structured metadata. Less structured information or modular, incomplete information about part of a resource can enrich structured metadata and enable additional functions. This book aims to highlight ways in which it is possible to think about metadata when building a collection of digital resources. Planning for digital library projects must more and more take into account the modularity of information and the multiplicity of data creators.

Organisation of this book

This book is intended to provide practical guidance on defining strategies to create and share metadata for digital resources. The applications that provide end-user access to these resources are here called 'digital libraries', although these systems are used in a variety of cultural heritage institutions and not solely in libraries. Part I of this book is this introductory chapter, which has outlined high-level issues relating to the role of metadata in cultural heritage institutions. Part II outlines key concepts related to metadata planning and the methods of metadata creation. Part III discusses in more depth the relationship of metadata decisions to systems design and functionality. Part IV focuses on interoperability of metadata; ensuring metadata can be re-used in new environments. Finally, Part V speculates to some degree on the future of metadata in the cultural heritage sector.

Notes

1. Caplan, P. (2003) *Metadata Fundamentals for All Librarians*. Chicago, IL: ALA Editions; p. 1.
2. Caplan, P. (2003) *Metadata Fundamentals for All Librarians*. Chicago, IL: ALA Editions; p. 3.
3. Rust, G. and Bide, M. (2003) 'The <indecs> metadata framework – principles, model and data dictionary'. Available at *http://www.eduworks.com/Documents/Workshops/EdMedia2003/Docs/indecs_framework.pdf*.
4. Dempsey, L. (2006) 'Registries: the intelligence in the network'. Post to Dempsey, L.'s blog, available at *http://orweblog.oclc.org/archives/001105.html*.
5. Bourda, Y. (2003) 'Définitions et concepts ; un exemple du processus de normalisation: les métadonnées pour les ressources pédagogiques'. Talk at the seminar 'Normes et standards pour les activités numériques dans l'enseignement', 9 October, 2003. Lyon, France.
6. See McLean, N. and Lynch, C. (2004) 'Interoperability between library information services and learning environments – bridging the gaps joint white paper on behalf of the IMS Global Learning Consortium and the Coalition for Networked Information'. Lake Mary, FL: IMS Global Learning Consortium; available at *http://www.imsglobal.org/digitalrepositories/CNIandIMS_2004.pdf*.
7. See Caplan, P. (2003) *Metadata Fundamentals for All Librarians*. Chicago, IL: ALA Editions.
8. Weibel, S. (1995) 'Metadata: the foundations of resource description', *D-Lib Magazine*, 1(1). Available at *http://www.dlib.org/dlib/July95/07weibel.html*.
9. Extensible Markup Language, maintained by the World Wide Web Consortium. See *http://www.w3.org/XML/*.
10. Standard Generalised Markup Language.
11. Resource Description Framework. See *http://www.w3.org/RDF/*.
12. See *http://www.tei-c.org/*.
13. Scalable Vector Graphics, XML-based graphic format maintained by the World Wide Web Consortium. See *http://www.w3.org/Graphics/SVG/*.
14. ContentDM. See *http://www.dimema.com/*.

Part II
Implementation of metadata creation activities

Cultural heritage institutions create metadata for a variety of purposes, such as information discovery and preservation. The missions of these institutions have evolved over time. They are increasingly creating and managing digital resources, sometimes with targeted projects, but more and more often as an integral part of their mission. A metadata creation policy can be defined either for a specific digital project (online delivery of a specific collection, a virtual exhibition, etc.) or at the level of the institution as a whole, as part of a general plan to manage digital resources.

The current digital library landscape is diverse, representing a great many metadata formats, terminologies, usage guidelines, and the like. It is important to thoroughly understand the roles of the different metadata types and standards in digital projects. Careful planning is required to determine the appropriate level of granularity for the metadata creation, appropriate metadata formats, and useful encoding guidelines.

The implementation of a metadata creation policy is deeply embedded in larger organisational issues. Frequently, metadata for a given set of materials is created by multiple persons, either because multiple staff positions exist to perform metadata creation simultaneously or because the personnel change over time. Regardless, it is important to guarantee a consistent practice among metadata creators, an appropriate level of quality of the metadata records, and a supportable model for maintenance of metadata records together with their digital objects. This requires the definition of a metadata creation strategy to manage the full metadata creation workflow.

Part II of this book aims to provide practical guidance on the implementation of metadata creation activities in a cultural heritage institution. Chapter 2 exposes the factors that must be taken into account in the choice of metadata formats. Chapter 3 describes the creation of metadata usage guidelines to guarantee a consistent metadata creation process. Chapter 4 focuses on the tools and methodologies to implement a metadata creation activity. Finally, Chapter 5 discusses the elaboration of a metadata creation strategy, including the development or mobilisation of the necessary competencies, the costs, and the management issues these strategies imply.

2

Choosing metadata standards for a digital library project

Metadata for a purpose

Metadata that is created should be useful. That statement sounds obvious, yet it is surprisingly difficult to put into practice. Metadata is expensive to create and record, and cultural heritage institutions should be cognisant of the benefits to discovery and management of data by the creation of robust metadata, while at the same time documenting related expenditures and balancing the benefits gained with the costs involved. The uses of metadata are not all immediate, however; institutions must think beyond currently-implemented systems and local environments to how metadata might provide services in next-generation systems, in aggregated environments, in contexts outside of cultural heritage institutions and in other knowledge domains.

While it of course is not possible to predict *all* future uses of metadata records, we can make educated guesses as to the sorts of functionality that might appear in the reasonably near future by examining the sorts of uses to which metadata is put today, and following emerging trends from a variety of communities. These current and future uses will be discussed later. For now, it is important to remember that all metadata recording should be undertaken with some defined purpose and user base in mind. The choice of metadata standards is one of the earliest decisions affecting that purpose, and the use to which metadata can be put immediately and in the future.

Factors to consider

Many complex and inter-related factors should be considered when selecting metadata standards to use for a digital library project. Factors related to the institution and its context, the standards themselves, the materials involved and the goals of the project all affect implementation decisions.

The institution

Different types of cultural heritage institutions, despite their similar goals, are surprisingly diverse in their resource description practices. Libraries, for the most part, conform to a shared cataloguing code and record format, and have a strong tradition of cooperative cataloguing to reduce the duplication of effort. Among cultural heritage institutions, library descriptive practices are the most standardised; however, despite all of these efforts, much diversity still exists. Archives, largely due to the fact that their holdings tend to be unique, have slightly less formal descriptive practices and little tradition of sharing information. The prevailing archival practice of multi-level description is largely absent from other types of cultural heritage institutions. Museums to an even greater degree lack prescriptive guidelines for metadata creation, and have little experience sharing records with peer institutions. Even the cataloguing process tends to be distributed in the museum environment, typically involving contributions from curators, registrars and collection information professionals in various capacities who all collect and record information about a museum's holdings.[1] Each of these communities has much to learn from the others about how best to describe resources in order to meet user needs, yet the important differences in mission and organisation among these different types of cultural heritage institutions will necessarily lead to different approaches in creating descriptive and administrative metadata. Metadata standards developed by your community or frequently used by institutions similar to yours are often a good choice, as they are likely to represent an approach to description or management already in use at your institution. Alternatively, choose a metadata standard more robust or specific than one common to your community if your project has more specific needs, but plan early for mapping to the community standard for interoperability reasons. (More on metadata mapping and interoperability can be found in Part IV.)

Within any given institution, the resources available to devote to metadata creation will also affect the choice of metadata standards. The sheer number of staff available for the task is an obvious factor, yet it is only one of many. The expertise and knowledge of that staff about the resources being described will affect the speed and depth of description possible, as will their familiarity with the metadata standards being used. Choosing metadata formats already in use at an institution has benefits such as quicker project start-up time, and easier cross-collection searching. The availability to an institution of appropriate authority lists for a given set of materials, workflows in place for automated metadata enhancement, and features of metadata creation systems intended to streamline data entry can all increase both production rates and quality of metadata being created, and thus affect the choice of metadata standards.

A metadata creation and delivery system already in use at an institution can restrict the metadata standards possible to choose from – many systems come pre-set with only a few options for descriptive metadata and little or no support for administrative or structural metadata, and many are not fully customisable to allow the use of other formats. This can create a vicious circle where an existing system dictates the choice of metadata standards for a new project, a body of records is created in that format, and any move to a new system and new (possibly more robust) formats then becomes more difficult due to problems with migration of the legacy data. The best defence against this cycle is good advance planning. Before selecting metadata creation systems, think ahead to the types of materials it will be used for and appropriate metadata standards for those materials. When using any implemented system, it is essential to think forward to how the metadata being created can be re-used and migrated into future formats.

The standard

The purpose, structure, context, and history of a metadata standard are also factors to consider when deciding if it is appropriate for a given project. Most metadata standards were created for some defined purpose: for example, a descriptive metadata structure standard might be intended for resource discovery for a particular knowledge domain, or metadata interoperability and discovery across domains. It might preference bibliographic description over archival description or the reverse. Analysis of the sort that David Bearman et al. performed as part of an early initiative to reconcile metadata requirements from the Dublin Core and INDECS/DOI communities will be a key factor in making a good decision; they state, 'The Dublin Core can be thought of as the HTML of Web metadata. It is crude by many resource description standards, an affront to the ontologists, and suffers some of the foibles of committee design. Notably, it is useful, and it is this useful compromise between formality and practicality on the one hand, and simplicity and extensibility on the other that has attracted broad international and interdisciplinary interest'.[2] Understanding issues such as these provides valuable context for making a choice among many possible metadata standards. Choose a standard that matches with the most specific purpose of your project; you can always map to less granular or specific standards for interoperability reasons, as described in Part IV.

Next, consider the technologies used to express a metadata standard. In the cultural heritage community, many metadata formats are defined with an XML DTD or a W3C XML Schema, and metadata conforming to the standard is expected to be expressed. Other standards are defined in RDF, and still others don't define a specific method of expression or provide multiple options. Other types of standards, such as controlled vocabularies, tend to be expressed using more specialised protocols. Choosing a standard expressed using technology that fits into an organisation's existing technological environment can significantly ease implementation. It is also useful to examine the body behind the creation or maintenance of a standard. Those endorsed by a national or international standards body, such as the National Information Standards Organization (NISO)[3] for the USA or the International Organization for Standardization (ISO)[4] internationally, carry with them the benefits of a public review process. Standards developed or maintained by a respected body in the cultural heritage community, such as the US Library of Congress,[5] suggest a certain degree of authority and sustainability. Those developed by members of a professional association representing a specialised community, such as the Visual Resources Association,[6] or those that arise out of a community of practitioners, such as the Digital Library Federation,[7] often carry the benefit of expert knowledge of the resources or technical environment for which the standard was intended. Metadata standards often progress through an extended beta or draft period during which they can be tested and refined. While often a beta or draft standard is the best choice for a certain aspect of a digital project (the draft standard in this case is likely fulfilling a function not currently well handled by other standards), first official releases of standards often contain significant changes from draft versions, which may require revising metadata after it was created if a draft standard was chosen. Consider also other factors such as how often a standard is updated (infrequently can mean the standard is in danger of being abandoned, too frequently can cause maintenance problems for metadata creators), and how many implementers a given standard has.

Ideally, the standards meeting all of a project's other criteria will fit well in an institution's existing technological environment, be officially endorsed, stable, and updated with reasonable frequency.

The materials

The materials themselves, especially their genre and format, are another primary consideration when selecting metadata standards. Materials of interest to specialised knowledge domains often have unique terminology by which users will access these materials. For example, 'classical' music is an adequate description for many general users of music, yet almost useless for the specialist. Similarly, for a general audience, the term 'rose' describing a flower in a picture may be adequate, while for a specialised botanical audience a formal Latin species name might be required. Some domains also possess specialised search requirements. Genealogical information might require searching on specific family relationships, chemical information might need to be searched by specific molecular compounds using the Hill notation system, or musical works might need to be searched by instrumentation or key. It is extremely difficult to create metadata that will simultaneously serve both specialised users in a given knowledge domain and casual generalist users. Digital project planners must decide early on which audiences will be the primary users of the material, and consequently choose metadata standards that support the terminological and discovery needs of the targeted users.

Even for generalist users, important differences exist between formats. Archival materials require a different approach to description than, say, scientific data sets (themselves a diverse lot). A text possesses different characteristics important for searching, such as language, than a historic photograph, for which location or persons pictured might be the primary information of interest to a user. Published materials similarly differ from unpublished materials: for example, unpublished materials often lack clear titles. Primary source materials require a greater focus on the circumstances of their creation than do secondary materials. Metadata for use of the material can also be important, for example, in the case of a sound recording where technical details of the format such as playing speed are essential. Multi-page objects and other materials may require user navigation within a given item; formats such as audio and video will require the creation of structural metadata in an appropriate standard. The bottom line is this: to adequately represent a given type of material, a metadata standard must possess elements in which essential characteristics can be recorded. First define what those essential elements are for a given project, and then choose standards that meet those needs.

The project

The specific objectives of a project also have a profound effect on the choice of metadata standards used. Most descriptive metadata standards popular in the cultural heritage community focus on item-level analysis, but multi-level description in the archival tradition is also possible by choosing standards that provide for it. If item-level description is desired, different metadata standards support description at different points on the continuum between short, simple, easy-to-create records and in-depth, robust, very granular records. Other factors, such as the repeatability of elements, the need to delineate multiple versions of a resource from one another, and the ability to create and maintain relationships between records, should also be considered when selecting metadata standards. Additionally, institutional and project needs for management of resources over time should be assessed in order to select appropriate administrative metadata standards.

Given all of these myriad factors affecting the choice of metadata standards, one might at this point wonder why metadata standards are important at all, and why an institution shouldn't just develop its own formats for recording the information needed for a given digital project. Occasionally, *very* occasionally, local development is a reasonable option – for example, when an institution has significant programming resources to devote to designing and making use of a local schema, and when the materials in question are significantly different in format or content than those of more mainstream collections, requiring a different approach to description or discovery. Designing and implementing a local format requires a significant investment of time, well beyond that required to implement already-existing standards. Using existing standards reduces (although it does not eliminate) the risk that needs will surface during a project that are not possible to meet with the standards in use. The decision as to whether to use an existing standard or build one's own should be made very carefully, and only after thorough consideration of all the implications.

Interoperability of metadata records with those from other institutions is another factor to consider when deciding which metadata standards to use, and whether or not to develop a new schema. Cultural heritage institutions can no longer afford to think only of how their resources will be used by patrons who walk in the door of their physical locations or on websites they maintain with their own institutional branding. In the networked world, it is no longer reasonable to expect that users will know about your site (or be able to find it in a search engine), then remember to visit it. Instead, the norm is now for cultural heritage institutions to push metadata (or allow it to be pulled) into any number of aggregated environments, including general Web search engines, broadcast search protocols such as SRU[8] and OpenSearch,[9] and metadata harvesting protocols such as OAI-PMH[10] to be used in services such as OAIster.[11] Services such as these can provide increased visibility and use for collections, but only if these collections can be found by users of the aggregations. Quality, shareable, interoperable metadata, as described in Part IV of this book, are key to this endeavour. For now, it is enough to say that diverging from standards makes interoperability more difficult.

Every metadata standard is necessarily a compromise. No one standard can be all things to all materials and to all users. When selecting

---

Box 2.1   **An alternate list of factors to consider when choosing a metadata standard**

UKOLN describes a similar but slightly reorganised taxonomy of factors to consider when selecting a metadata standard:

- purpose of metadata;
- attributes of resource;
- design of standard;
- granularity;
- interoperability;
- support;
- growth;
- extensibility;
- reputation;
- ease of use;
- existing expertise.

Source: UKOLN (2004) 'Choosing a metadata standard for resource discovery' (*http://www .ukoln.ac.uk/qa-focus/documents/briefings/briefing-63/html/*).

standards for a given project, it is important to balance the need for generality with that for specificity. Select a standard that allows you to be as granular, complete, and consistent as you can afford and justify with services to your users. You can always map your master metadata to other less-structured and less-granular standards at a later time for inclusion of your metadata in shared environments. This process will be described in greater detail in Part IV.

Functions of metadata standards

It is easy to get caught up in thinking about descriptive metadata. Often, a team planning a digital project will congratulate themselves on their well thought-out decision on which descriptive metadata standard to use, and forget that there are many other types of standards that will be needed for the same project. Most digital projects will have discovery, delivery, and preservation needs that require several metadata standards to work together. Each of these standards should be carefully chosen.

Metadata standards can be categorised in many different ways. One of the most common divisions is outlined in Priscilla Caplan's book, *Metadata Fundamentals for all Librarians*.[12] Such categorisations are useful, but no matter what the grouping, it's likely some standards will not fit neatly into a single category. This section will present a loose categorisation of metadata standards focusing primarily on the role the standard will play in a digital project. Standards from each of these categories should be considered as part of the project planning process, and a standard fulfilling that function should be chosen if it is necessary for that project. The standards listed here are illustrative of the types of standards in this category – these lists are by no means comprehensive.

Descriptive metadata structure standards

These are standards that list elements considered to be important for describing a resource, including both its physical characteristics and its intellectual content. These standards are those that cultural heritage professionals tend to be the most familiar with. This information is the sort that a user searches or browses on, or reads in a display for an item he has already found, to determine if it is one he is interested in. What many initially tend to think of as 'metadata' is the type of thing found as elements in descriptive metadata structure standards: title, creator, subject, and so on. These standards typically specify which elements are required, which are repeatable, and what order the elements can appear in. Many of these standards also include some elements for the physical or digital carrier that resource appears on, blurring the line somewhat with technical metadata. Occasionally, they will delve slightly into the realm of content standards by suggesting or requiring a way in which a value for a specific element should be presented. Dublin Core is a simple descriptive metadata structure standard, intended for use with any type of resource, that is in wide use in the cultural heritage community. Several other descriptive metadata structure standards intended for general use exist, along with countless options intended for use for a specific type of material.

Some general descriptive metadata structure standards are:

- MARC Bibliographic (*http://www.loc.gov/marc/bibliographic/ecbdhome. html*)
- MARCXML (*http://www.loc.gov/marcxml/*)
- MODS (*http://www.loc.gov/mods/*)
- Dublin Core (*http://www.dublincore.org*)

Some specialised descriptive metadata structure standards are:

- VRA Core, Version 4.0 (*http://www.vraweb.org/projects/vracore4/*). Visual resources.
- CDWA Lite (*http://www.getty.edu/research/conducting_research/ standards/cdwa/cdwalite.html*). Art and architecture.
- GEM (*http://www.thegateway.org/about/documentation/metadata Elements*). Learning objects.
- IMS Learning Resource Metadata (*http://www.imsproject.org/ metadata/*). Learning objects.
- ETD-MS (*http://www.ndltd.org/standards/metadata/current.html*). Electronic theses and dissertations.
- DDI (*http://www.ddialliance.org/*). Datasets in the social and behavioural sciences.

Content standards

Content standards are standards that provide rules for the syntax of an entry into a metadata field. Their purpose is to promote consistency among metadata records to allow better search and discovery for users. As Priscilla Caplan has put it, '... metadata schemes without content rules are not very usable'.[13] Murtha Baca agrees, stating, 'Unless the metadata elements of data structure are populated with the appropriate data values (terminology), the resource will be ineffectual and users will not be able to find what they are looking for, even if it is actually there'.[14] Content standards are often used with descriptive metadata structure standards, but can also be applicable to other types, for example, a standard for how to format dates will be useful for recording technical metadata. The cultural heritage sector has produced several large-scale content standards, covering the formulation of many different types of metadata elements. Smaller standards also exist for many individual types of content, such as dates or identifiers. These smaller-scale standards are often *syntax encoding schemes*, which provide rules for how to formulate a value, or *vocabulary encoding schemes* (also known to the cultural heritage sector as controlled vocabularies), which define a set (although often large) of terms from which a value must be chosen. Syntax encoding schemes are used when the possible values for an element are infinite and would benefit from a consistent structure (such as dates), and vocabulary encoding schemes are used when some sort of a controlled vocabulary (such as a subject heading list, thesaurus, or classification scheme) is desired. The library community is familiar with content standards and their relationship with metadata structure standards by way of AACR2 and its relationship to MARC. Even so, the distinction between the two is not always clear. Choosing and adhering to appropriate content standards for relevant elements is an essential part of creating consistent, quality, and useful metadata.

Some large-scale content standards are:

- AACR2 (*http://www.aacr2.org/*)
- Cataloging Cultural Objects (CCO) (*http://vraweb.org/ccoweb/cco/*)
- Describing Archives: A Content Standard (DA:CS) (*http://www .archivists.org/catalog/pubDetail.asp?objectID=1279*)

Some smaller-scale content standards:

- Archival Moving Image Materials: A Cataloging Manual (*http://www.itsmarc.com/crs/arch0332.htm*). Supplement to AACR2 for cataloguing moving image materials.
- W3CDTF (*http://www.w3.org/TR/NOTE-datetime*). Syntax encoding scheme for dates.

- DOI (*http://www.doi.org/*). Syntax encoding scheme for identifiers.
- DCMI Type Vocabulary (*http://dublincore.org/documents/dcmi-type-vocabulary/*). Vocabulary encoding scheme for resource types.
- AAT (*http://www.getty.edu/research/conducting_research/vocabularies/aat/*). Vocabulary encoding scheme for subjects for art and architecture.

Markup languages

Markup languages differ from the other types of metadata standards described here in that they mark up actual content; that is, they surround data that makes up the document itself with small pieces of metadata indicating the meaning and/or function of that part of the document content. One of the most widely-known markup languages in the humanities is the Text Encoding Initiative (TEI), a markup language defined first in SGML, then later in XML. The TEI consists of tags defining the structure, criticism, and interpretation of texts of all sorts, including prose, verse, drama, speech, dictionaries, and so on. Encoded Archival Description (EAD), although sometimes referred to as a descriptive metadata structure standard, is perhaps more correctly categorised as a markup language. EAD was developed to encode archival finding aids using any depth of multi-level description, and by design is flexible enough to be able to provide markup on a finding aid in virtually any existing structure. Its tag set is designed more to highlight individual structural elements as they happen to appear, rather than to specify in advance elements that should be recorded. By this definition, EAD is more appropriately a markup language than a descriptive metadata structure standard, although the finding aid itself is a form of metadata about an archival collection. Markup languages are useful in digital projects where searching within the actual content of material (for example, for a line of verse or a specific musical passage) is a priority, in addition to or in place of metadata-based searching.

Some markup languages include:

- TEI, P5 (*http://www.tei-c.org/P5/*)
- EAD (*http://www.loc.gov/ead/*)
- MusicXML (*http://www.recordare.com/xml.html*)
- MathML (*http://www.mathmlcentral.com/*)

Authority data

Authority data standards hold vocabulary encoding schemes, such as those for subjects and names. These standards do not define specific vocabularies, but are rather the structure in which a vocabulary defined elsewhere is stored and used by digital library systems. Most contain a method for specifying a main term and other terms the main term should be used in place of. Some provide means for making robust connections between terms. These standards provide various ways of recording contextual and administrative data about terms, influenced in each case by the intended use of standard. While authority data is usually accessed internally by a digital library system to enhance cataloguing or searching and browsing, rather than being exposed directly to users, the use of standards for encoding and storing authority data is still beneficial for exchanging authority data among institutions, and can save some development time by enabling the re-use of programming code to interact with a standard format.

Some authority data standards are:

- MARC Authority (*http://www.loc.gov/marc/authority/ecadhome.html*)
- MADS (*http://www.loc.gov/standards/mads/*)
- EAC (*http://www.iath.virginia.edu/eac/*)
- SKOS (*http://www.w3.org/2004/02/skos/*)

Administrative metadata

This catergory is perhaps the broadest one included here, encompassing metadata for technical management of resources, rights management, long-term preservation, processing history, and any other administrative purpose. Many categorisations of metadata standards break administrative metadata into subcategories; here, it is enough to think of these standards as those that help an institution to manage digital resources. Information of this sort is often stored in a proprietary format in a digital asset management software system. In this case, some of the decision-making work in selecting appropriate standards has been undertaken already. However, it is important as part of the project planning process to assess the scope of the administrative metadata created and stored by the software system. Project planners should ensure the specific pieces of data suggested by relevant standards are all being stored, and that this data is available for export in a format that can be made to conform with standards, for exchange of data between systems and migration to future systems. Administrative metadata is easy to forget about, but ensuring during the project planning stages that it *is* created, and created well, is essential for persistence of digital material over the long term.

Some administrative metadata standards include:

- MIX (*http://www.loc.gov/standards/mix/*). Technical metadata for digital still images.
- PREMIS (*http://www.oclc.org/research/projects/pmwg/*). Preservation metadata for any type of content.
- ODRL (*http://odrl.net/*). Rights expression language.

File formats and embedded metadata

Often a digital project will use file formats with embedded metadata. This metadata can be of any type, and the type and depth of this metadata is generally influenced by the main audience(s) for the file format. In addition to file formats with native support for embedded metadata, Adobe has developed the Extensible Metadata Platform (XMP) for embedding RDF/XML documents directly into digital files,[15] which is gaining increasing support in multimedia applications. Embedding metadata within a content file has the benefit of this metadata travelling with the content as it moves between systems, making it less likely the object will become orphaned or separated from its context. However, using *only* metadata embedded in a file can severely restrict the options a project has for the metadata it records, as few if any file formats allow the full range of metadata required for discovery and management of resources to be embedded. It is therefore the safest option to both make use of a file format's capability to embed metadata and to store full metadata separate from the digital object. The work undertaken to ensure the two remain in sync over time should be worth the benefits received from using both approaches simultaneously.

Some file formats with embedded metadata are:

- JPEG2000 (*http://www.jpeg.org/jpeg2000/*). Administrative and descriptive metadata are defined by an extension.
- TIFF (*http://partners.adobe.com/public/developer/tiff/index.html*). Mostly administrative metadata with a few descriptive elements, and an area for private use.

- Broadcast WAVE (*http://www.ebu.ch/en/technical/publications/ userguides/bwf_user_guide.php*). A small number of administrative and descriptive metadata elements are available in the 'broadcast audio extension chunk'.

- MP3. Some documentation is available at *http://www.mp3-tech.org/*. Descriptive metadata can be embedded within MP3 files in formats such as ID3 (*http://www.id3.org/*).

Wrapper standards

These are metadata schemes that pull together content and various types of metadata into a single bundle. They are useful for bringing together all versions of a digital object and its metadata for ingestion into a digital repository, or for sharing objects among institutions. Wrapper standards tend to include a method for specifying *structural metadata*, which indicates the relationships between different versions of content, parts of content to the whole, and metadata to the content to which it applies. Structural metadata can be essential for providing navigation within and between versions of a digital object for end-users.

Some metadata wrapper and structural metadata standards include:

- METS (*http://www.loc.gov/mets/*)

- MPEG-21 DIDL (ISO/IEC TR 21000-2 and ISO/IEC TR 21000-3)[16]

- SMIL (*http://www.w3.org/TR/SMIL2/*). Developed as a multimedia presentation format, but can be used as a metadata wrapper standard.

Using multiple standards

Given the many different types of metadata standards and the similarly diverse functions they support, it is reasonable to expect more than one, perhaps even several, types of metadata standards could be used for any given digital project. So how does one put them together?

In some cases, some of the work has already been undertaken. Certain metadata standards make a conscious effort to include more than one type of metadata, for example, MPEG-7,[17] which covers both descriptive and administrative metadata for audiovisual materials, including what are known as 'low-level' features such as camera motions. Many others focus on just one type, but also happen to include elements that could be categorised as another type. Even with standards that don't fit entirely within one of the categories listed here, it is extremely likely no one standard will meet the entire needs of any given project.

Application profiles

Application profiles[18] are methods that allow metadata creators to combine elements from multiple formats as needed. The term application profile grew out of the Dublin Core community, and Dublin Core as a 'core' metadata standard tends to provide elements of use to many different application profiles. While this method would seem to promote interoperability by encouraging the re-use of elements from existing standards whenever possible, application profiles have gained only limited adoption in the cultural heritage community. A number of factors may have contributed to this lack of adoption, including the increasing popularity of XSLT-based metadata mappings between metadata standards expressible in XML as an interoperability mechanism, the sharp rise in the number of standards available making it more likely an existing standard would be appropriate as-is, and the cultural heritage community's general preference for XML (in which it is slightly harder to mix and match metadata elements from multiple schemes) over RDF (in which it is easier to do this).

Some examples of application profiles are:

- ViDE DC Application Profile (*http://www.vide.net/workgroups/videoaccess/resources/vide_dc_userguide_20010909.pdf*)

- DC-Library Application Profile (*http://dublincore.org/documents/library-application-profile/*)

- DC Collection Application Profile (*http://dublincore.org/groups/collections/collection-application-profile/*)

While the ability to pull all relevant metadata elements into a single document via a mechanism like an application profile is attractive, it is not always necessary or sometimes even desirable. Digital asset management systems can and should do the grunt work of managing the different types of metadata associated with a digital object or group of objects, regardless of whether this metadata is stored in a single document or many. Wrapper standards can be used internally by these systems or externally when sharing metadata to bind documents using different metadata standards together as necessary. Choosing one metadata standard does not preclude the use of others; rather, several are usually needed, working together, to provide the discovery, delivery, and management functions necessary for a robust and sustainable digital project.

Notes

1. Coburn, E. (2007) 'Beyond registration: understanding what cataloging means to the museum community', *VRA Bulletin*, 1(34).
2. Bearman, D., Rust, G., Weibel, S., Miller, E. and Trant, J. (1999) 'A common model to support interoperable metadata', *D-Lib Magazine*, 5(1). Available at *http://www.dlib.org/dlib/january99/bearman/01bearman.html*.
3. National Information Standards Organization (*http://www.niso.org/*).
4. International Organization for Standardization (*http://www.iso.org/*).
5. Library of Congress. 'Standards at the Library of Congress'. Available at *http://www.loc.gov/standards/*.
6. Visual Resources Association (*http://www.vraweb.org/*).
7. Digital Library Federation (*http://www.diglib.org/*).
8. Library of Congress. 'SRU: Search/Retrieval via URL'. Available at *http://www.loc.gov/standards/sru/*.
9. OpenSearch, A9. See *http://opensearch.a9.com/*.
10. Open Archives Initiative. 'Open Archives Initiative protocol for metadata harvesting'. Available at *http://www.openarchives.org/pmh/*.
11. OAIster (*http://www.oaister.org*).
12. Caplan, P. (2003) *Metadata Fundamentals for All Librarians*. Chicago, IL: ALA Editions.
13. Caplan, P. (2001) 'International metadata initiatives: lessons in bibliographic control'. Paper presented at the Conference on Bibliographic Control in the New Millennium, Library of Congress, 15–17 November 2000. Washington, DC: Library of Congress; available at *http://www.loc.gov/catdir/bibcontrol/caplan_paper.html*.
14. Baca, M. (2003) 'Practical issues in applying metadata schemas and controlled vocabularies to cultural heritage information', *Cataloging & Classification Quarterly*, 36(3/4): 47–55.
15. Adobe. 'Extensible Metadata Platform (XMP)'. Available at *http://www.adobe.com/products/xmp/*.
16. International Organization for Standardization (Various) 'ISO/IEC 21000-2:2005. Information technology – Multimedia framework (MPEG-21) – Part 2: Digital Item Declaration', 2nd edn (2005) and 'ISO/IEC 21000-3:2003. Information technology – Multimedia framework (MPEG-21) – Part 3: Digital Item Identification', 1st edn (2003).
17. For an MPEG-7 overview, see *http://www.chiariglione.org/mpeg/standards/mpeg-7/mpeg-7.htm*.
18. Heery, R. and Patel, M. (2000) 'Application profiles: mixing and matching metadata schemas', *Ariadne*, 25: available at *http://www.ariadne.ac.uk/issue25/app-profiles/*.

3

Creating metadata usage guidelines

Continuing to plan

Choosing which metadata standards to use is only the first step in metadata planning for digital projects. Many more decisions must be made before getting started actually creating metadata. The next steps after choosing metadata standards are generally defining and testing usage guidelines for those standards. Even the most prescriptive types of metadata standards, for example, the AACR2 content standard, contain optional rules and some ambiguity, and most metadata standards are not nearly this prescriptive. Carefully planning and documenting usage guidelines for the metadata standards selected for a digital project will lead to more consistent metadata, and therefore better services can be provided based on that metadata.

Making decisions that are reflected in metadata usage guidelines should be a collaborative process. In order to ensure the metadata created fulfils its purpose, a variety of perspectives is necessary, including those from experts in metadata creation; user needs; the systems being used to create the metadata, store the content over the long term, and deliver it to end-users; the subject matter of the resources; and budgeting and project management issues. The syntax of the actual values entered into metadata elements has as much to do with the services that can be provided based on those values as the selection of the metadata elements themselves. A team of individuals that together possess a clear vision for the functionality a digital project should provide and the means to deliver that functionality is necessary for a successful project. The size of this team will necessarily vary with the size of the project and the size of the institution; ensuring the appropriate perspectives are represented is the goal, regardless of how many individuals it takes to provide those perspectives.

When making decisions about the usage of each element in the metadata standards selected, base these decisions on the function the information in that element will perform. Guidelines for recording information in a metadata element will differ based on whether that data will be used for browsing, structured searching, keyword searching, display to a user as supplemental information, linking, or management functions such as the generation of statistics. The most cost-effective metadata creation procedures are those that provide only that information for which there is a reasonable (if not immediate) use. Avoid as much as possible filling in elements or structuring data in a particular way *only* because it appears in a standard or other implementers do it that way. Instead, find out what the reason for the inclusion of that element is, or review the other implementer's procedures, and determine if those goals apply to your project.

Documentation of metadata usage guidelines will be useful as a procedural manual for the individuals creating metadata, as part of more comprehensive project documentation and for planning future projects. Writing guidelines is difficult, however. Different individuals who might use these guidelines might benefit from different levels of detail and different organisational schemes. No one single document will be the perfect tool for all individual metadata creators, yet it is both possible and worth the effort to attempt to find a happy medium of detail and conciseness that will provide a reasonable manual for use by diverse staff. The Collaborative Digitisation Program's *Dublin Core Metadata Best Practices*[1] is an excellent model for an appropriate compromise in level of detail. However, it is important to note that the Collaborative Digitization Program's guidelines were originally intended for a large group of institutions with a diverse set of materials all contributing to a central resource, and were only later released to the public in recognition of the potential applicability of these guidelines to many further institutions. They therefore are necessarily not very prescriptive. Local guidelines for a more constrained set of materials and for use in a more constrained environment can and probably should be more prescriptive, with the goal of creating more consistent metadata. The *Minnesota Metadata Guidelines for Dublin Core Metadata Training Manual* shows how specific these guidelines can be, utilising system screenshots.[2]

Topics to cover in metadata usage guidelines

Metadata usage guidelines can be organised and constructed in many different ways. The exact procedure to follow when creating this documentation will necessarily differ among institutions and projects. However, there are a set of topics that will likely be common to many of these projects, representing decisions project planners should make in advance of any actual metadata creation activity.

Why the guidelines and the project exist

Even if metadata creation staff have no other role in the project, they deserve the opportunity to know why their work is important. Metadata usage guidelines tend to be fairly long and verbose, so give those who must follow those guidelines an understanding of what the benefits will be from doing so: for example, for searching or management of digital resources. Inevitably, cases will arise where the guidelines don't cover what to do in a given situation. High-level context provided for the metadata usage guidelines will help metadata creation staff make decisions in these cases that conform to the goals and spirit of the project.

Explanation of when each record must stand on its own

Much of the metadata created as part of a digital project will need to stand on its own, as a single record divorced from those around it, in certain situations. In these cases, metadata usage guidelines need to specify that data needs to be explicitly entered into every record even when it repeats information from the previous record. Entering 'same as above' or " " (quotation marks indicating 'ditto') into a descriptive metadata record that may be displayed to a user without the 'previous' record will both confuse the user and make searching less effective. Not all metadata needs to be duplicated in all records, however. The very nature of multi-level description, such as that recorded in EAD, implies an inheritance of properties from higher levels into lower levels. Systems making use of multi-level description for search, display, or metadata sharing should be able to make use of this inheritance, and therefore instructions to duplicate higher-level data in lower levels should *not* appear in metadata usage guidelines. A similar principle may also apply for information that applies to an entire collection. Depending on the functionality of the systems involved in generating, storing, and searching metadata, it may be possible to record certain information (such as a rights statement) that applies to an entire group of materials only once, yet perform search, display, and metadata sharing functions as if that information were actually present in the record for each item. Investigate these possibilities early in the project planning process, and write metadata usage guidelines to take advantage of any functionality of this type that will be implemented.

Indication of the metadata standards in use

Seasoned metadata creation personnel will benefit from knowing the base standards on which metadata usage guidelines operate, so as to apply their existing expertise in these standards. Novice metadata creation personnel can use this information to learn more about the standards and the specific application decisions made for this project, both of which will help them in this project and in the future. Links to usage guidelines for specific metadata standards can help reduce the size of project metadata creation guidelines, although one must be careful not to require too much moving back and forth between resources as part of the metadata creation process.

Definition of what is being described

For all types of metadata being created, especially descriptive, technical, and rights metadata, decide up front and document in metadata usage guidelines exactly what should be described if the material exists in multiple versions. For example, if the materials in the collection have been digitised from analogue originals, the metadata creator must know whether a record (or an individual element within a record) describes the intellectual content of the resource, its analogue carrier, or any of its digital carriers.

Which metadata is generated automatically and which is recorded by a human

Even though usage guidelines are largely intended as a procedural manual for human metadata creators, it is useful for those humans to know what other metadata is being generated by other means such as those described in Chapter 4. Providing this information contributes to the understanding of the project as a whole by metadata creation staff, educates the staff about the possibilities for automated metadata generation, and minimises the risk of duplication of information between automatically- and human-generated metadata. These explanations are particularly important for types of metadata likely to be largely automatically generated, such as technical metadata. If metadata creation staff know which elements are being generated behind the scenes, they can be confident that no essential information is being left out. In cases where a human is performing manual enhancement of metadata produced by automated means, for example, computer matching of names against an authority file or a basic OCR and automated markup of a text, knowing how that automated step was performed will help the human better know when to question the results of the automated work and when to trust it.

Element definitions

If the element definitions from the metadata standards in use are not prohibitively long, it is useful to include them in local metadata usage guidelines. The standard definitions should be clearly marked as such, and followed by any local constraints or further embellishment on the official definitions, also clearly delineated as such. It is important, however, not to change the definition of a metadata element in a local environment such that metadata created according to the local guidelines creates conflicts with the officially sanctioned definition of that element. If changes to an element definition of this scope would be required, it is better to make use of the built-in extension mechanisms present in some metadata standards, develop a small local schema to supplement the standard being used, or choose a different standard entirely that better meets the project needs.

Cardinality rules for each element

Indicate in project metadata usage guidelines whether or not each element is required, and how many times it may appear. Repeating elements to accommodate multiple values is generally best practice, so usage guidelines should clearly instruct metadata creators to follow this procedure when possible. Project metadata usage guidelines should include information on the cardinality rules for the element *for this project*, rather than only those from the standard itself. A local project should not develop guidelines that violate cardinality rules from a standard, but the project may place further restrictions beyond those required by the standard, such as considering an element required for the local implementation when the standard considers it optional, or recommending a maximum number of times a given element should be used when the standard declared an element repeatable as desired.

Content standards and encoding schemes that apply to each element

While it is appropriate to include information about content standards that apply to the entire metadata creation process in the introductory material for metadata usage guidelines, it is rare for it to be appropriate to use a single content standard for all metadata elements being recorded as part of a digital project. Large-scale content standards such as AACR2 can contain instructions that apply to many elements, however their scope tends to extend only to descriptive metadata, and other standards (such as the W3CDTF syntax encoding scheme for dates) may be more appropriate for specific elements. For each element, metadata usage guidelines should indicate which content standard, syntax encoding scheme, or vocabulary encoding scheme (controlled vocabulary) should be used when formulating the metadata value. Occasionally, no external content standard will apply; in this case, provide guidance in the documentation. The exact nature of the instruction will vary based on the nature of the metadata element. For some elements, an instruction to transcribe information directly from an item should be sufficient. For others, a link to a controlled vocabulary (or inline list if it is very short) might be appropriate. For still others, a description of the appropriate syntax, such as 'recording playing time in minutes' may be enough.

Desired granularity of records and individual elements

Metadata usage guidelines should indicate the granularity of information appropriate to meet project goals at several levels. The first level is for the record as a whole, which is generally achieved as described above by indicating which metadata fields are required. In addition, providing the metadata creator with information on how the information in the optional fields will be used will help that person determine for themselves when to fill in these optional fields. Granularity guidance should also be given for individual metadata elements. For free-text descriptive fields, document the level of detail this description should contain. Provide guidance on the most specific level of geographic information (country, city, etc.) that should be provided, and how (if at all) hierarchy above that level should be indicated. For subject access, indicate how broad or specific chosen index terms should be. Also provide an indication as to how important a feature must be in a resource to warrant noting in the metadata record. Determine the appropriate depth of indexing that meets project goals, and balance this need with the funds available for metadata creation. For projects including applying a markup language to content, the depth of markup desired should be determined ahead of time and documented for use by project staff. For example, if a project involves using TEI to mark up the full text of letters, a basic structure delineating the salutation from the body and closing material might be suggested, along with guidelines for which features found within the body should be encoded beyond a basic paragraph structure, such as geographic places and personal names, and for which elements the encoder should provide normalised versions of the text.

Appropriate sources of information and their use

Some content standards, such as AACR2, define a 'chief source of information' from which data for a given element should be taken. In cases where a content standard in use doesn't prescribe this, metadata usage guidelines might provide some guidance to the metadata creator on where to find information for use in a specific element. Often there will be no restriction necessary, and the metadata creator should be free to use all resources at his or her disposal, including reference sources, to determine the information that should be recorded. In this case, usage guidelines should provide some direction on the amount of effort that should be spent looking for this information, possibly in terms of time spent, number of resources consulted, or the depth of information expected to be provided. Consider the case where it is desirable to identify all individuals pictured in a historical photograph. Individual metadata creators will have different levels of research expertise, but to remain cost-effective, some practical limit should be put on the amount of research undertaken to provide the information in any given metadata element. Determine this limit by balancing the project goals achieved by recording information with the funds available for metadata creation.

Most projects will fall somewhere in the great middle between only using information available on the item itself and exhaustive research to authoritatively discover all information possible to record in the selected metadata standards. Record these decisions in the metadata usage guidelines for the project.

Syntactic details

Low-level details such as the use of capitalisation, punctuation, abbreviations, and initial articles should be prescribed in project metadata usage guidelines. Some content standards prescribe these details, but it is useful to comment on them within your local guidelines to save metadata creators time moving back and forth between multiple resources to meet project guidelines for such low-level details. While most modern search systems can handle variations in most of these low-level details, other functions such as browsing may benefit from their consistent treatment. Developing and adhering to guidelines for these details has another, less tangible, benefit as well. There are many cases where a user interface might display data from multiple fields or multiple records in close proximity, for example, in a title browse list or a brief results display. Maintaining consistency across records and fields with regards to these low-level details presents a more unified display, and can help to instil in a user confidence that the metadata he is viewing is of high quality. Consistency among low-level details such as these is relatively easy to achieve, and simply makes metadata *look* better, even if it has a negligible effect on most system functionality.

Use and development of controlled vocabularies

The use of controlled vocabularies can often help to achieve project goals for structured searching and browsing functionalities. Metadata usage guidelines should indicate and provide lists or links to controlled vocabularies for all metadata elements for which they are appropriate. These controlled vocabularies can be small, externally maintained lists, such as the DCMI Type Vocabulary,[3] large, collaboratively-developed lists such as the NACO-developed name authority list,[4] or locally-maintained vocabularies. In all cases, metadata usage guidelines should cover the case in which a concept, name, or the like is needed but is not available in the controlled vocabulary to be used with a given metadata element. Sometimes the appropriate action is to simply look for a way to record this information elsewhere in the record. For vocabularies that are cooperatively- or locally-developed, an institution may choose to put resources towards enhancing those vocabularies as part of the metadata creation process for a given project. This policy would take project resources, but would help to ensure a more robust vocabulary for all users in the future. If vocabulary enhancement is desired, metadata usage guidelines should include information on how that enhancement should be executed. Even with vocabulary enhancement techniques, it is common to want to include a value not under authority control in a field in which authority control is appropriate. Every effort should be made to provide a machine-readable distinction between those values under authority control and those that are not. Information on techniques for achieving this distinction can be found in Chapter 4. A set of metadata records for which specific elements contain values under authority control in most but not all cases reduces the functionality that can be provided on those values that are authority controlled. Avoid placing both authority controlled and non-authority controlled values in the same field without any indication of which is which.

This is a long list of decisions to make, all before you get to see any benefit from making them, but the planning process doesn't have to be overwhelming. Patterns should emerge in the policy decisions made – for example, names can and in most cases should be treated the same way whenever they appear. Don't worry about missing important instructions in the first draft of the guidelines; using an iterative writing and testing process can help ensure all important areas are covered in the end.

Writing, testing, and refining usage guidelines

Once preliminary decisions are made regarding metadata entry issues, the work of turning these decisions into actual metadata usage guidelines can begin. In addition, gathering and examining samples of metadata usage guidelines for other projects, such as those in Box 3.1, can provide additional ideas for what to include and how to present the information.

Box 3.1 Some metadata usage guidelines

- California Digital Library Online Archive of California Best Practice Guidelines for Encoded Archival Description (*http:// www.cdlib.org/inside/diglib/guidelines/bpgead/*)

- CanCore Guidelines for the Implementation of Learning Object Metadata, Version 2.0 (*http://www.cancore.ca/en/guidelines.html*)

- Collaborative Digitization Program: Dublin Core Metadata Best Practices, Version 2.1 (*http://www.cdpheritage.org/cdp/ documents/CDPDCMBP.pdf*)

- Descriptive Metadata Guidelines for RLG Cultural Materials (*http://www.rlg.org/en/pdfs/RLG_desc_metadata.pdf*)

- Digital Library Federation/Aquifer Implementation Guidelines for Shareable MODS Records (*http://wiki.dlib.indiana.edu/confluence/ download/attachments/28330/DLFMODS_ImplementationGuide lines_Version1.pdf*)

- IN Harmony Sheet Music from Indiana Cataloging Guidelines (*http://www.dlib.indiana.edu/projects/inharmony/projectDoc/ metadata/inHarmonyCatalogingGuidelines.pdf*)

- Kentuckiana Digital Library Production Guide, Version 2.0 (*http://kdl.kyvl.org/html/kdl/guidelines.htm*)

- Metadata Guidelines for Digital Georgetown (*http://digital .georgetown.edu/pdf/metadata.pdf*)

- Metadata Guidelines for Geospatial Datasets in the UK. Part 2. Creating Metadata using UK GEMINI Version 1.0 (*http://www .gigateway.org.uk/pdf/guidelines/MetadataGuidelines2.pdf*)

- Minnesota Metadata Guidelines for Dublin Core Metadata Training Manual (*http://www.bridges.state.mn.us/bestprac/training.pdf*)

- National Library of Australia Guidelines for the Creation of Content for Resource Discovery Metadata (*http://www.nla.gov .au/guidelines/metaguide.html*)

- New York Public Library Picture Collection Online Metadata Guidelines (*http://digital.nypl.org/mmpco/docs/metadata.pdf*)

- University of Virginia Metadata Documentation (*http://www.lib .virginia.edu/digital/metadata/*)

Perhaps the most difficult part of writing metadata usage guidelines is determining how much information to include in the procedural manual. Frequent linking to external resources can create too much moving around between different documents, which can slow the metadata creation process, but too much detail in a single document addressing cases that only apply rarely can similarly slow the process. It is impossible to cover in pre-written guidelines all possible scenarios metadata creation staff might encounter. Endeavour to address the common cases in the documentation, and provide enough context as to why the procedures are the way they are to enable staff to make good decisions when scenarios not explicitly covered arise. The testing process for metadata usage guidelines described below can help inform a reasonable balance for the specific project in question.

While all element descriptions in a set of metadata usage guidelines should include some indication of how data should be entered, another way to streamline the size and flow of metadata creation procedures is making good use of tools in a metadata creation system itself to ensure consistency and quality of data entry. Features in a metadata creation interface such as limiting entered values to a pre-determined list, easy selection of values used in previously-entered records, and enforcement of specific data types (such as dates) are extremely valuable to streamline the metadata creation process and will likely help produce higher-quality records. Metadata usage guidelines should be written with these features in mind, indicating to metadata creation staff when the system will help them with data entry, when the system might automatically change data that has been manually entered, and when special care should be taken with data entry because the system is not able to assist with enforcement of project guidelines. In cases where the system can assist in entering an appropriate value, the metadata usage guidelines may not need to be as verbose in instructing the metadata creator in the usage of an element.

Good layout and organisation are essential in effective procedural manuals for metadata creation. It should be obvious to users of the guidelines where they are in the structure of the document and which element is being discussed at all times. Page headers, section numbering, and consistent typography throughout the document can help to achieve this goal. Many metadata usage guidelines are structured according to individual metadata elements in the order metadata creation staff encounter them. Consider, however, that not all metadata creation staff will choose to enter elements in the same order. Grouping elements by function or data type may also help eliminate duplicate instructions and keep the manual to a reasonable size.

In their role as a procedural manual, the guidelines should contain only that information a given set of metadata creation staff needs to do their work. As described in Chapter 4, many different metadata creation workflows are possible, most of which do not involve a single person creating all the metadata for the entire digital project. Create a different set of metadata usage guidelines for each part of the metadata creation workflow; for example, if digitisation staff create technical metadata and a different set of staff create descriptive metadata, create two different procedural manuals so that each set of staff has simple, easy access to the instructions needed to complete their work.

Examples are an essential part of effective metadata usage guidelines. Be careful with them, however, as they can also be misleading. No matter how often and how well metadata creation staff are reminded not to 'catalogue to the examples' but to also read and understand the text of the guidelines, examples are powerful tools that are easy to simply copy without considering all of the seemingly boring, extraneous text. Use real-world cases for examples as much as possible, showing common situations. Examples of rare cases or exceptions serve more to distract than to assist. Provide concise examples showing the principle in question and just enough context so that the example makes sense – rarely are full records necessary inline as part of the text itself. Full record examples as an appendix, referenced separately, are appropriate, however, and also extremely useful. Good examples take a great deal of time to create, but their benefit for metadata creation activities of any reasonable scale greatly outweigh the up-front time in planning.

Once a first draft of project metadata usage guidelines has been created, the next step is to test them. This step is absolutely essential, as even the most experienced individuals will not write absolutely complete, consistent, and coherent guidelines on the first try. If possible, have someone who has not yet been involved with the project try the guidelines out with the actual metadata creation system to be used and some actual materials from the target collections. Carefully consider all reports of areas of concern from this test; writing the first draft of metadata usage guidelines is a long and involved process that will likely result in the authors becoming attached to the text and proud of their work (and rightly so). Guidelines that make sense only to their authors, however, are of little use when others are to be the ones making use of them. Even in cases where those that will do the actual metadata creation work were involved in the writing of the guidelines, background information, assumptions, and intent not documented are quickly forgotten. The goal of testing metadata usage guidelines is to ensure all relevant information has been documented.

Once an initial round of testing has been undertaken, check the revised guidelines carefully. Wherever a change has been made, check that this change hasn't caused any internal inconsistencies. Ensure the examples exactly match the instructions in the text – there's nothing worse than guidelines where the text says one thing and the example another. Proofread carefully; errors in small details like formatting, spelling, and capitalisation don't instil confidence in the value of following the guidelines presented. Most projects don't have time for a second (or third, or fourth ...) test of metadata guidelines, but take advantage of any extra time that appears to review and revise them as much as possible before they are put into production.

Even with the best planning, no set of metadata usage guidelines will be perfect. Be prepared to revise them once the project actually starts and the guidelines are being used in a production environment. Develop a procedure for metadata creation staff to easily note problems they encounter ahead of time, and at the same time create a workflow for actually addressing these problems. Don't instil too much bureaucracy into this process – waiting a significant amount of time for a decision on a problem that has arisen requires placing a resource aside and returning to it later, a situation best avoided if at all possible. Empower your metadata creation staff to participate meaningfully in the process of adding to or revising the guidelines; after all, they are the ones that use them every day. Participative technologies such as Wikis[5] can provide appropriate platforms on which to build a reporting and revision workflow for metadata usage guidelines. These guidelines are the key to creating consistent, quality metadata; give them a level of attention appropriate to their importance to a digital project.

Notes

1. Collaborative Digitization Program Metadata Working Group (2005) 'Dublin Core Metadata Best Practices Version 2.1'. Available at *http://www .cdpheritage.org/cdp/documents/CDPDCMBP.pdf*.

2. Quam, E. (2002) 'Minnesota Metadata Guidelines for Dublin Core Metadata Training Manual'. Available at *http://www.bridges.state.mn.us/bestprac/training.pdf*.

3. DCMI Usage Board (2006) 'DCMI Type Vocabulary'. Avaliable at *http://dublincore.org/documents/dcmi-type-vocabulary/*.

4. Library of Congress. 'Name Authority Cooperative Program of the PCC'. Washington, DC: Library of Congress; available at *http://www.loc.gov/catdir/pcc/naco/naco.html*.

5. Wikipedia entry on 'Wiki'. Available at *http://en.wikipedia.org/wiki/Wiki*.

Creating metadata

The metadata creation process

Creating metadata is almost never as simple as one individual sitting down with an item and recording a few of its features into a system designed expressly for this purpose. The many different types of metadata created for different purposes may require multiple individuals and multiple systems to create. For some types of metadata, user interfaces designed for quick data entry with a minimum of errors are most appropriate. For others, direct use of XML editors might be the most streamlined approach. Metadata from sources other than manual creation by project staff is often useful and must be seamlessly integrated into a digital project's workflow. A thorough metadata quality control procedure is a key but often neglected component of a successful digital project. All of these factors must be considered when designing a metadata creation process. Careful planning before metadata creation begins will help to ensure consistent, high-quality metadata that meets a project's defined goals.

Designing a metadata creation workflow

There is no one single metadata creation workflow that is best for all digital projects. Designing a good metadata creation workflow for your project begins with an analysis of the source of the data for each metadata element, then the organising of these elements into logical groups based on how they will be created, and when. It is not always necessary or even desirable to create metadata in an order suggested by a specific metadata standard. Metadata creation does not have to be a linear process whereby one record is complete before the next one is begun. It also does not have to be an entirely human-driven process. A strong movement has arisen in the cultural heritage sector towards 'making data work harder', to achieve discovery and delivery goals in a more cost-effective and useful manner.[1] A metadata creation workflow may integrate information created by humans, pre-existing from other sources, automatically generated from content, and created by automatic enhancement methods working on existing metadata.

For metadata to be created by humans, determine which project staff members are best suited to completing which types of metadata. Some technical and structural metadata may be best entered by digitisation staff while they are performing digitisation duties. Some descriptive metadata that involves transcribing information from an item, or general knowledge, might be suitable to be undertaken by less senior staff. Descriptive metadata requiring in-depth subject analysis or specific domain expertise could be added as enhancements to a preliminary record at a later time, as could authority control for appropriate fields. Examine carefully which metadata elements will have values identical for each item in a collection, or for easily identified large subsets of the collection. Such information is best entered once and either replicated to or inherited by records for individual items. Determine which of your project staff is most qualified to generate this information, and also decide whether entering it before item-level metadata creation begins will help staff creating item-level records to see their context – or if this information would just be in the way and is best suppressed or not even generated until the end of the project. Plan your ideal workflow to put the appropriate metadata elements in front of the appropriate staff members at the appropriate time to make the metadata creation process as cost-effective as possible.

Integrating pre-existing metadata into your metadata creation workflow can greatly increase the cost-effectiveness and efficiency of a digital project. If any machine-readable metadata already exists for the materials in question, look for creative ways to make use of it. This could include item- or collection-level MARC records, word-processed or HTML finding aids, spreadsheets with collection inventories, holdings data, and so on. Also look for pre-existing data from outside your institution, and outside the cultural heritage sector. Publishers, vendors, and even enthusiastic users often have metadata that may be of use to your project. Don't automatically discount metadata from these types of sources as unreliable or non-authoritative. Do an objective review of when a given metadata source can be used as the basis, either by automated or by human means, of metadata that meets your project goals. Any of this pre-existing metadata that can be mapped cleanly into the target metadata standards should be processed and loaded into the project's systems before manual metadata creation begins. Even when pre-existing metadata does not map cleanly into the desired format, it is useful to make this information available to metadata creation staff.

Various automated metadata generation methods may also help to streamline a project's metadata creation workflow. In projects involving full text, OCR or re-keyed material from scanned page images is generally provided before human markup begins. In some cases, it may be possible to apply basic automated markup to the text, such as identification of headings and marking of page breaks, before the text is presented to a human for markup. Some projects may benefit from automated textual analysis, either to be used as-is or given to a human for review. The Automatic Metadata Generation Application (AMeGA) project at the University of North Carolina, Chapel Hill is a high-profile project that studied various automatic generation methods for descriptive metadata. The AMeGA final report[2] briefly summarises automatic metadata generation techniques, notes that at this time there exists a '*disconnect* between experimental research and application development', (p. vii) and comments that even in experimental systems, research is 'generally limited to specific subject domains, resource types, resource formats, and metadata elements' (p. 5). Nevertheless, some effective automated metadata generation techniques already exist for specific circumstances, and their use and effectiveness is likely to grow. Projects now in the planning stages may well be able to make effective use of these techniques.

Technical metadata in particular is well suited to automatic generation. Tools such as JHOVE[3] can be used to generate a significant amount of technical metadata from a digital object. Human effort could then be used to provide only that technical metadata that is not possible to automatically generate from a digital file, for example settings used in scanning software. RLG Programs' now inactive Automatic Exposure initiative has worked to standardise technical metadata generated by imaging devices in the hope that this metadata could be more easily integrated into digital preservation systems.[4]

Automated metadata enhancement techniques are those that are performed on some kind of existing metadata with the goal of standardising the syntax of certain fields or performing analysis on this metadata similar to that undertaken on a complete text. While these tools are starting to find their way into production, mostly in metadata aggregators that deal with diverse metadata from many sources, in many cases they may also be of use to individual metadata creation projects. Syntax normalisation routines can be fairly simple; for example, the California Digital Library has released a Java-based date normalisation tool,[5] which identifies and normalises the syntax of dates appearing in various parts of a Dublin Core record, with the goal of using the normalised dates for searching. Tools such as these are useful for taming pre-existing metadata created without strict content guidelines. Syntax normalisation routines can also be more complex and interact with authority files or other data sources containing a list of values which data is normalised against. One such project came from Johns Hopkins University, which has experimented with routines that attempt to automatically match names from transcribed statements of responsibility for sheet music with names in the NACO authority file, with an accuracy rate of 58% overall, and 77% when the correct name exists in the authority file.[6] Tools such as these can help cut down the cost of metadata creation by focusing expert human effort on reviewing their output, leaving transcription duties to less expert staff. Tools going beyond syntax normalisation to actual content analysis are beginning to emerge as well. A growing number of projects have been experimenting with subject clustering and classification techniques, such as the California Digital Library's American West project,[7] the Digital Library Federation-sponsored *The Distributed Library: OAI for Digital Library Aggregation*,[8] and Emory's MetaCombine project.[9] These subject-clustering techniques seem to be most effective for providing high-level browse access to collections, a function not well supported by traditional controlled vocabularies from the cultural heritage sector.

After considering all of the potential sources of metadata for your materials, examine the capabilities for supporting your ideal workflow of any metadata creation systems that are being considered or are already in place at your institution or for this project. While many factors affect the choice of a metadata creation system – most notably the fact that most are part of a larger digital asset management system that provides an entire suite of functions – the more a system is configurable to support a desired workflow, the better. Bring the ideal metadata workflow to the table when the choice of metadata creation systems is being discussed, and ensure that the cost-effectiveness gained by streamlined workflows are considered as important factors when determining which metadata creation systems to use for a digital project.

If you do have to compromise from your ideal workflow, and it is likely you will to at least some extent, all is not lost. It is usually still possible to make customisations to metadata creation interfaces designed to speed metadata creation and help ensure adherence to project guidelines.

User interfaces for metadata creation

A well-designed user interface for metadata creation can significantly streamline the metadata creation process (Figure 4.1). The system behind this user interface would then be able to generate metadata records that conform to the metadata standards chosen for the project. However, no one design can or will work for all projects, even if they use the same base metadata standards. Tailoring a metadata creation interface for your specific project can make metadata creation more cost-effective and help reduce errors. If your content management system allows you to customise metadata creation screens, or if you are designing your own metadata creation system, it is often well worth the time spent in the planning process enhancing the functionality of these systems. If your system provides the capability to customise the metadata creation

Figure 4.1 A metadata creation interface specifically designed for sheet music (note the feature making it easy to re-use names already in the system)

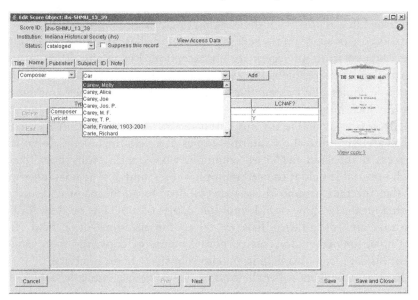

process differently for different groups of materials, you can tailor the metadata entry process even further. If not, a reasonable compromise between flexibility and functionality must be reached. In any case, making use of a trained user interface specialist can help any project get the most out of its metadata creation tools.

There is no single overall design that is always better than others. Depending on the complexity of the project metadata model and the experience of the metadata creation staff, sometimes a tabbed view or other method for breaking the interface into logical groups of related fields will be preferable. In other situations, making all fields a given user will need to fill in appear on a single screen could lead to greater productivity. Like metadata usage guidelines, user interfaces for metadata creation should be designed such that each individual making use of the metadata creation system has access to all of the functionality he needs, but no more. User interfaces should support the specific workflow designed for a project, separating, for example, descriptive from technical metadata when different staff members are responsible for their creation. It may be appropriate to allow or disallow an individual access to metadata he is not directly responsible for creating; depending on the nature of the project and of the staff, this information may either help that individual do his work or distract him from it. ImageTag from Cornell University[10] is an example of a specialised metadata creation tool that facilitates pagination and feature identification of page images at crucial points in a project workflow, as described in a report from the Making of America IV project.[11]

Good use of space on the screen is helpful in all types of interfaces, and metadata creation interfaces are no exception. Repeatable fields pose a particular space problem for metadata creation interfaces – providing multiple copies of all repeatable fields takes up an enormous amount of room which might rarely be used and still enough copies of a given field might not be available for any given record. Yet requiring the user to take extra action to show multiple copies of a field might slow down the process if repeated fields are common. Consider carefully how likely each repeatable field is to need multiple values, and design a default view of the interface around those expectations. In addition, provide users with a means to show or hide multiple copies of a field as needed. Radio buttons and drop-down lists to refine the meaning of a field, for example, for personal versus corporate names or copyright date versus creation date, can also help in maximising space in an interface.

Interface 'widgets' – small tools to help the user quickly achieve a certain function – can be extremely effective in metadata creation interfaces. Widgets can make it easy to enter values from controlled vocabularies, and add terms to these controlled vocabularies when necessary and appropriate, without opening too many extra windows. Increasingly, access to controlled vocabularies is being integrated into metadata creation systems, rather than asking metadata creation staff to go to outside systems or print resources to locate controlled vocabulary terms. OCLC, for example, has integrated access to 11 frequently-used controlled vocabularies (and more are planned) into the Connexion cataloguing interface using the Microsoft Research Task Pane.[12]

Additional features such as tabbing between fields, automatic completion of frequently or previously used values, and drop-down lists for small controlled vocabularies can all speed data entry. Other widgets can assist in enforcing adherence to project guidelines. Dates, for example, might be expected to always be entered as four digits. In this case, the metadata creation system could check as data is entered that only digits are present, and could provide next to that field radio buttons to indicate if the date is approximate, inferred, or questionable, if such indication is within the scope of the project. Record validation, checking that required fields are completed and all fields conform to any machine-readable restrictions, should be available to the user at any time, and should be performed automatically when a record is saved or otherwise navigated away from. These features shouldn't be intrusive, however. There may be many valid workflow reasons for setting aside a record in progress, and the metadata creation interface should not discard any information entered to that point or enforce more work on a record than is possible at that moment. Design the metadata creation interface to support actual workflow for your project.

Many other features can be added to metadata creation interfaces to aid in the construction of quality metadata. Jane Greenberg of the University of North Carolina at Chapel Hill has undertaken significant research into metadata creation interfaces. One user study Greenberg's team performed on a metadata creation tool resulted in the following revisions to the first version of the interface:

- development of an online tutorial;
- addition of guidelines for applying subject elements;
- present required metadata elements at the top of the data entry screen and optional elements at the bottom;
- addition of secondary data entry screens for entry of items related to the primary item being described.[13]

Although this study was completed on an interface designed for use by resource authors, who tend to be novice metadata creators, many principles from user studies of this sort are applicable to metadata creation interface design for experts as well.

After any interface customisations have been made, test the interface with the project metadata usage guidelines and actual materials for which metadata will be created. Actual users are a key source of information on how an interface should function. Take feedback from this test and make good faith efforts to address any concerns raised. It may not be possible within your technical environment to address every issue; look for creative solutions. By making the metadata creation process as easy and error-free as possible, metadata creation staff can focus on their true intellectual work instead of struggling with their data entry tool.

Creating metadata directly in XML

The majority of metadata standards commonly used in the cultural heritage sector are designed to be expressed in XML (maintained by the World Wide Web Consortium, or W3C).[14] In some cases, creating metadata in these standards directly in XML is preferable to using a graphical interface: for example, when encoding content using a markup language. Creating metadata or marking up a document in XML is best undertaken using software packages called XML editors. While XML can be created in any text-editing software, including packages such as Microsoft Word, TextEdit for Mac, or WordPad for Windows, most implementers prefer to use XML-aware applications, either XML plug-ins for generic text editors or software packages specifically designed for XML editing (Box 4.1).

XML editors contain a number of features designed to assist the user with creating XML files. The most important of these are ensuring that the XML file is well formed and valid. XML editors generally contain a feature that allows the user to check at any time if the current XML document is well formed, and receive a report outlining where any formedness errors may be. More advanced editors contain features such as automatic generation of a closing tag when an opening tag is typed, and automatic generation of a closing quote on an attribute when an opening quote is typed, designed to remind the user that the closing feature is necessary and save him a bit of typing. Some editors contain the option to turn features such as these off for more advanced users who find them distracting. Ensuring validity of an XML document to its target format works in a similar manner. The XML document itself

Box 4.1   Choice of an XML editor

Commonly-used XML editors in the cultural heritage sector include Oxygen, XMetal, and XMLSpy. jEdit and eMacs are open source alternatives.

Some criteria to take into account when selecting an editor are:

- validation/well-formedness checking;
- user-friendliness of interface;
- unicode support;
- XSLT-to-HTML result display;
- XSLT application mechanism;
- PDF export;
- support for programming languages.

contains a reference to the target DTD or Schema defining the XML format, as described in more detail in the next section. The XML editor uses this reference to check the XML document against the target format, and report errors it finds.

Many XML editors include other helpful features in addition to the basic well-formedness and validity checking. To assist with the creation of well-formed files, some editors provide automatic indentation of nested tags to visually indicate hierarchy of the document. Others use colour-coding to visually indicate the structure of the document and assist with locating syntax errors, by showing element names, element values, attribute names, and attribute values all in different colours. Some editors can make use of XML catalogs,[15] which promote interoperability of XML files by mapping simple references to a W3C XML Schema or DTD to the actual location of the schema or DTD files on the local computer or network, eliminating the need to explicitly reference a local or locally-networked copy of a schema or DTD within the XML document. Often editors will provide means for easily adhering to a declared schema or DTD by providing quick entry of elements and attributes with constrained values, and on-the-fly checking of entered element and attribute values against the expected data type. Some software packages provide editing views that substitute a more graphical representation of the tags in an XML document for the native view using angle brackets. The more feature-rich the editor and the more skilled its user, the faster XML markup can be performed. For projects that will require creation of raw XML, selecting a good XML editor and investing in training will generally pay off with greater efficiency in metadata creation.

Benefits of learning XML technologies

Virtually all digital projects should involve at least one staff member familiar with a variety of XML technologies, as many systems that store and manage digital collections make use of XML, and many metadata standards likely to be used in the cultural heritage sector are expressed in XML. However, understanding the basic tenets of XML, such as opening and closing tags, attributes, character entities, and appropriate nesting, will not usually be sufficient for creating and managing robust metadata. In order to implement a metadata standard expressed in XML, an understanding of the languages in which XML formats are defined is necessary to understand the elements defined and how they fit together.

Currently, three major methods exist to define an XML format and provide a means for software to validate an XML instance document to ensure its structure and data conform to that format. The oldest of these is the Document Type Definition (DTD).[16] DTDs were first used with SGML,[17] then later adapted for use with XML. DTDs are relatively simple documents that define element names and cardinality, basic data types, relationships between elements, and attributes. Some of the older, more established metadata standards in the cultural heritage sector grew into XML from original versions in SGML.[18] Most of these formats, such as TEI and EAD, are still defined with DTDs, which have over time been migrated from SGML to XML. When an XML document conforms to a DTD, the XML document must contain a DOCTYPE declaration indicating the DTD that should be used to validate the document.[19] For example, an EAD file conforming to the EAD2002 DTD would include the following DOCTYPE declaration as its first line:

```
<!DOCTYPE ead PUBLIC "+//ISBN 1-931666-00-8//DTD
ead.dtd (Encoded Archival Description (EAD) Version
2002)//EN" "ead.dtd">
```

The second method for defining an XML format is the W3C XML Schema.[20] XML Schema language is significantly more complex than

DTDs, but it provides a few advantages over DTDs. XML Schemas are themselves XML documents (whereas DTDs are not), making it easier to use the same tools to read and manage schemas as XML instance documents. XML Schema language provides more control over datatypes than do DTDs, and provides more robust features for embedding documentation into the schema files. Metadata standards developed recently in the cultural heritage sector tend to use XML Schemas to define the standard: for example, MODS and METS. Dublin Core's XML representation is similarly defined by an XML Schema.[21] XML instance documents conforming to a format specified by an XML Schema must include an attribute on the root element pointing to the namespace and location of the target schema. For example, an XML document conforming to version 3.2 of the MODS XML Schema would include the following attribute on its root element:

```
xsi:schemaLocation="http://www.loc.gov/mods/v3
http://www.loc.gov/standards/mods/v3/mods-3-
2.xsd"
```

The third language for defining XML formats is the newest option, known as RELAX NG.[22] RELAX NG can be expressed in either of two syntaxes (XML and non-XML compact), each of which is significantly less verbose than XML Schema syntax. To date, RELAX NG has been more popular for use in defining document formats and markup languages than for true metadata formats, and is currently used more frequently in business than in the cultural heritage sector. Both the DocBook[23] and OpenDocument[24] formats are defined in RELAX NG.

Although the three formats contain significant differences, they are increasingly being used interchangeably. The new P5 release of TEI will allow users to choose any of the three formats for validation of TEI files.[25] EAD is now available as a W3C XML Schema and a RELAX NG schema in addition to the original DTD.[26] Tools such as Trang[27] allow conversion of one of these three formats to another, although the conversion is not always lossless due to differences in the capabilities of each of the formats. Most XML editors can provide a graphical representation of the structure of an XML format defined through one or more of these three languages. Using this feature can often help one learn the structure of these languages or a new metadata format they define more quickly.

In addition to understanding the languages in which XML formats are defined, it is valuable for digital project planners and metadata specialists to gain some experience with other XML technologies as well. The most useful of these are XSLT and XPath. XSLT is the XML language used to transform XML documents into other XML documents and into other non-XML document formats.[28] XPath is the language used to locate nodes in an XML document, and is used within XSLT to indicate which part of the XML document should be processed. One primary use of XSLT in digital projects is to map one XML-based metadata standard to another, described further in Chapter 10. Understanding the way in which these mappings are performed using XSLT can help during the planning process, allowing project planners to see more clearly how implementation decisions will affect metadata interoperability down the road. The other primary use of XSLT, transforming XML files for presentation in formats such as HTML and PDF, is also valuable in project planning and implementation. Transformation of metadata stored in XML does not have to be completed only for end-users at the very end of a project; quick-and-dirty transformations can be completed on the fly at any point in the lifecycle of a project, on any number of records. Transformations from XML into presentation formats can be useful as part of the planning process, allowing planners to see a variety of possible ways metadata that is created could be used. XSLT transformations are also helpful during the process of metadata creation by showing staff doing XML encoding what the results of various encoding practices might be, and can be used as part of the metadata quality control process.

Quality control for metadata creation

The definition of 'quality' in library cataloguing has received a great deal of attention in the library literature, representing a variety of perspectives on the issue.[29] Historically, studies of cataloguing quality have typically focused on 'accuracy' (by some definition of the term) such as typographical errors[30] and conformance to cataloguing rules. More recently, this definition has expanded in the library realm to include *utility* of records.[31] In a diverse metadata environment, quality must be interpreted in the broadest sense, and in fact, there is no one single definition that will work for all digital library projects. As R. John Robertson states, 'That different settings and purposes require different types of metadata quality should be no surprise as there are already other domains of knowledge management which have very different standards and purposes'.[32]

Shreeves et al. provide a framework in which metadata is analysed in light of two high-level 'information quality (IQ) categories': intrinsic IQ, aspects 'that can be assessed by measuring attributes of information items themselves in relation to a reference standard', and relational/contextual IQ, aspects 'that depend on relationships between the information and some aspect of its usage context'.[33] Another influential definition is outlined as a set of seven characteristics by Thomas Bruce and Diane Hillman, which are more granular than the framework used by Shreeves et al.:

- **Completeness.** Description is as complete as is feasible; as many elements are applied as possible.

- **Accuracy.** Description is correct and factual, and adheres to appropriate syntax rules and vocabularies.

- **Provenance.** Circumstances under which metadata was created and subsequent transformations that have been performed.

- **Conformance to expectations.** Degree to which metadata meets the expectations of a defined community.

- **Logical consistency and coherence.** Element usage adheres to standard definitions of a community, and elements are applied and presented consistently.

- **Timeliness.** Metadata changes keep up with resource changes, and up-to-date metadata is available for distribution together with a resource.

- **Accessibility.** Metadata can be read and understand by users.[34]

An early study of the quality of Global Information Locator Service (GILS; *http://www.gils.net*) metadata standard overseen by William E. Moen conducted an extensive literature review of metadata quality factors, and discovered the following factors used in previous projects: access, accuracy, availability, compactness, comprehensiveness, content, consistency, cost, data structure, ease of creation, ease of use, economy, flexibility, fitness for use, informativeness, quantity, reliability, standard, timeliness, transfer and usability. The GILS study used factors under the headings of completeness, profile, accuracy and serviceability in its final analysis.[35]

Implementing structured quality control procedures into metadata creation workflows is absolutely essential for a successful digital project. Traditional library cataloguing workflows tend to have simple quality control procedures, involving expert review of individual records created by less experienced staff or an outsourcing vendor.[36] In today's technological environment, many options exist in addition to simple individual record review for the creation of an efficient and effective quality control workflow.

The design of a complete quality control workflow begins not from a record-centric perspective, but rather from a use-centric perspective – defining quality metadata records as those that enable systems to fulfil the purposes for which they were designed. Think of what a record can do, rather than thinking of it as an artefact in and of itself. It is still a difficult task to translate this high-level perspective, and other theoretical quality factors such as those defined by Bruce and Hillmann, into concrete, practical workflows that can be used in a production environment. Work by Naomi Dushay and Diane Hillmann in the context of the National Science Digital Library (NSDL) project analysing metadata quality problems can provide a useful means of connecting features of metadata records to the purpose they serve in a project, sorting record quality errors into the following categories: missing data, incorrect data, confusing data, and insufficient data.[37] Developing checks that look for errors in each of these categories can help to ensure a metadata quality control process provides adequate coverage.

Understanding various strategies for implementing quality checks is the first stage in translating overall goals into specific workflow steps. Not all quality control must be completed by a human. Automated checks can be performed on every single record with minimal human intervention, and are most effective on objective data that can be algorithmically verified as correct. Manual review is almost always impractical to perform on every record; a small sample, performed by someone other than the person who originally created the metadata, will catch systematic problems in the creation process and the occasional simple mistake. It is important to remember that no quality control procedure can be perfect. Errors will always creep in, no matter how many times you go over every single record with a fine-toothed comb. A systematic quality control process using both automated and manual means confirms that metadata records on the whole fulfil their purpose, rather than promising the entire metadata repository is completely error-free.

Several levels of quality checking can be performed on individual records. The first level is syntactic, and generally can be performed by automated means, often as the record is being created rather than after the fact. Checks of this sort can confirm that all required fields contain data, that all data in the record conforms to the syntax rules for the field in which it appears, and that all values in a field requiring conformance to a controlled vocabulary actually match a value from that vocabulary. The next level of quality checking for individual records is slightly more abstract, involving more subjective criteria. Checks of this sort might ensure that metadata is created at the appropriate level of granularity, that the appropriate resource is represented in the metadata record, that elements are used properly, that records are 'complete' to expectations beyond simple rules for requiring fields, or that subject analysis has been performed at the expected level. Even with subjective criteria, only check against those expectations outlined in your metadata creation guidelines; it is ineffective and overall a poor policy to be checking records according to criteria not made clear to metadata creation staff.

Checking individual records is an integral part of a complete quality control program, but it is not enough by itself. Higher-level views of metadata records showing trends that appear across records are required to check additional aspects of metadata quality. These high-level views might demonstrate how often a field is used, how many times a field appears in the average record, how many fields have data in the average record, or how many unique values are present for a given field in a set of records. They could also display a de-duplicated list of all values appearing in a given field or set of fields across the database. Simple reports can be effective means of viewing the nature of a group of metadata records, locating quality problems, and preventing problems from becoming systematic. One example of a report of this sort might display an alphabetical, de-duplicated list of all values in a particular field along with a count of how many records that field appears in, to help identify authority control errors or assess subject analysis choices. Dushay and Hillmann describe a method for reviewing large groups of metadata records that goes a step beyond simple database reporting, using commercial visual graphical analysis software.[38]

Metadata quality control is an iterative process that never ends. Even after initial metadata creation is complete, record editing may continue. Once a set of content is made available to end users, reports are likely to come in pointing out errors or questioning the appropriateness of metadata in a given record. A procedure must be in place to review and respond to these reports using the same quality metrics as the original metadata creation. In addition, each time metadata is repurposed for a new use, such as for aggregation (see Part IV), a quality review must be performed to ensure metadata records support the new intended use. Robust review procedures and clear documentation will make this process easier, especially if significant periods of time have elapsed since initial metadata creation.

Notes

1. Dempsey, L. (2005) 'Making data work harder'. Post to Dempsey, L.'s blog, available at *http://orweblog.oclc.org/archives/000535.html*.
2. Greenberg, J., Spurgin, K. and Crystal, A. (2005) 'Final report for the AMeGA (Automatic Metadata Generation Applications) project', Washington, DC: Library of Congress; available at *http://www.loc. gov/catdir/bibcontrol/lc_amega_final_report.pdf*.
3. Harvard University. 'JHOVE – JSTOR/Harvard object validation environment'. Cambridge, MA: Harvard University; available at *http://hul. harvard.edu/jhove/*.
4. Research Libraries Group (2004) 'Automatic Exposure: capturing technical metadata for digital still images', available at *http://www.rlg.org/longterm/ ae_whitepaper_2003.pdf*.
5. California Digital Library. 'Date normalization utility', available at *http://www.cdlib.org/inside/diglib/datenorm/*.
6. Patton, M., Reynolds, D., Choudhury, G.S. and DiLauro, T. (2004) 'Toward a metadata generation framework – a case study at Johns Hopkins University', *D-Lib Magazine*, 10(11). Available at *http://www.dlib.org/dlib/ november04/choudhury/11choudhury.html*.
7. TopicSeek and CDL (2005) 'Metadata Enhancement Feasibility Study Final Report'. Oakland, CA: California Digital Library American West project; available at *http://www.cdlib.org/inside/projects/amwest/cdl_clustering OAI_final.pdf*.
8. Newman, D., Hagedorn, K. and Landis, B. (2006) 'Clustering, classification, and metadata enhancement techniques', Presentation at Metadata Enhancement and OAI Workshop, 24–25 July 2006, Atlanta, GA. Available at *http://www.metascholar.org/events/2006/meow/viewpaper.php?id=3*.
9. Krowne, A. and Halbert, M. (2005) 'An initial evaluation of automated organization for digital library browsing', in *Proceedings of the 5th ACM/IEEE-CS Joint Conference on Digital Libraries (Denver, CO, USA, June 07–11, 2005)*. New York, NY: ACM Press, 2005; pp. 246–55. Available at *http://doi.acm.org/10.1145/1065385.1065442*. See also MetaScholar Initiative (2004) 'MetaCombine Project Interim Report – mid-point project report on experiments at Emory University in combined searching, automated organization of OAI and Web resources, and new forms of scholarly communication', The MetaCombine Project, available at *http://www.metacombine.org/reports/project/MetaCombine- Interim-Report-final.doc*.
10. Cornell Institute for Digital Collections. 'Sources', available at *http://cidc. library.cornell.edu/source/*.
11. University of Michigan Digital Library Services (2001) 'Assessing the costs of conversion – Making of America IV: The American Voice 1850–1876'. Ann Arbor. MI: University of Michigan; available at *http://www.umdl. umich.edu/pubs/moa4_costs.pdf*.
12. Vizine-Goetz, D., Houghton, A. and Childress, E. (2006) 'Web Services for controlled vocabularies', *Bulletin of the American Society for Information*

Science and Technology, June/July: available at *http://www.asist.org/ Bulletin/Jun-06/vizine-goetz_houghton_childress.html*.

13. Greenberg, J., Crystal, A., Robertson, W.D. and Leadem, E. (2003) 'Iterative design of metadata creation tools for resource authors', in Sutton, S., Greenberg, J. and Tennis, J. (eds) *Proceedings of the 2003 Dublin Core Conference: Supporting Communities of Discourse and Practice – Metadata Research and Applications*. Seattle, WA: Dublin Core; p. 5.

14. W3C World Wide Web Consortium (*http://www.w3.org*).

15. Walsh, N. (2001) 'XML Catalogs – Committee Specification 06 Aug 2001', *OASIS*, available at *http://www.oasis-open.org/committees/entity/spec.html*.

16. W3 Schools. 'DTD tutorial', available at *http://www.w3schools.com/ dtd/default.asp*.

17. For more information on SGML and its relationship to XML, see Caplan, P. (2003) *Metadata Fundamentals for All Librarians*. Chicago, IL: ALA Editions.

18. For a history of moving TEI from SGML to XML, see Bauman, S., Bia, A., Burnard, L., Erjavec, T., Ruotolo, C. and Schreibman, S. (2004) 'Migrating language resource from SGML to XML: the text encoding initiative recommendations', in *Proceedings of the Fourth International Conference on Language Resources and Evaluation*. Paris: ELRA; pp. 139–142. Available at *http://www.tei-c.org/Activities/MI/lrec04-teimigr504.pdf*.

19. The entire DTD can also be embedded in the <!DOCTYPE> itself, but this is an uncommon method for metadata in the cultural heritage sector.

20. W3 Schools. 'XML Schema tutorial', available at *http://www.w3schools. com/schema/default.asp*.

21. The Dublin Core Usage Board has approved encodings for Dublin Core in HTML/XHTML, XML, and RDF/XML. The current recommended XML syntax for both simple and qualified Dublin Core can be found at *http:// www.dublincore.org/documents/2003/04/02/dc-xml-guidelines/*, although a new syntax, known as DC-XML, is currently under development – see *http:// dublincore.org/architecturewiki/DCXMLRevision/DCXMLMGuidelines*.

22. Clark, J. and Murata, M. (2001) 'RELAX NG Tutorial Committee Specification 3, December 2001', *OASIS*, available at *http://relaxng.org/ tutorial-20011203.html*.

23. Walsh, N. (2006) 'The DocBook Document Type Committee Specification, 02 June 2006', *OASIS*, available at *http://www.oasis-open.org/committees/ download.php/19151/docbook-4.5-spec-cs-03.html*.

24. Durusau, P., Brauer, M. and OpperMann, L. (2006) 'Open Document Format for Office Applications (OpenDocument) v1.1 Committee Draft2, 24 Jul 2006', *OASIS*, available at *http://www.oasis-open.org/committees/ download.php/19321/OpenDocument-v1.1-cd2.pdf*.

25. Text Encoding Initiative Consortium. 'TEI: The P5 release', available at *http://www.tei-c.org/P5/*.

26. EAD2002 schema, see *http://www.loc.gov/ead/eadschema.html*.

27. Thai Open Source Software Center. 'Trang – Multi-format schema converter based on RELAX NG', available at *http://thaiopensource.com/relaxng/ trang.html*.

28. W3 School. 'XSLT Tutorial', available at *http://www.w3schools.com/xsl/ default.asp*.

29. Thomas, S.E. (1996) 'Quality in bibliographic control', *Library Trends* 44(3): 491–505.
30. Beall, J. and Kafadar, K. (2004) 'The effectiveness of copy cataloging at eliminating typographical errors in shared bibliographic records', *Library Resources and Technical Services*, 48(2): 92–101.
31. Starr Paiste, M. (2003) 'Defining and achieving quality in cataloging in academic libraries: a literature review', *Library Collections, Acquisitions & Technical Services*, 27: 327–38.
32. Robertson, R.J. (2005) 'Metadata quality: implications for library and information science professionals', *Library Review*, 54(5): 295–300.
33. Shreeves, S.L., Knutson, E.M., Stvilia, B., Palmer, C.L., Twidale, M.B. and Cole, T.W. (2005) 'Is 'quality' metadata 'shareable' metadata? The implications of local metadata practice on federated collections', In Thompson, H.A. (ed) *Proceedings of the Twelfth National Conference of the Association of College and Research Libraries*, 7–10 April 2005, Minneapolis, MN. Chicago: Association of College and Research Libraries; pp. 223–37. Available at *http://www.ala.org/ala/acrl/acrlevents/shreeves05.pdf*.
34. Bruce, T.R. and Hillmann, D.I. (2004) 'The continuum of metadata quality: defining, expressing, exploiting', in *Metadata in Practice*. Chicago: American Library Association; pp. 238–56.
35. Moen, W.E., Stewart, E.L. and McClure, C. (1998) 'Assessing metadata quality: findings and methodological considerations from an evaluation of the US Government Information Locator Service (GILS)', in *Proceedings of the Advances in Digital Libraries Conference*. Washington, DC: IEEE Computer Society; pp. 246–255.
36. Lam, V.-T. (2005) 'Quality control issues in outsourcing cataloging in United States and Canadian academic libraries', *Cataloging & Classification Quarterly*, 40(1): 101–22.
37. Dushay, N. and Hillmann, D.I. (2003) 'Analyzing metadata for effective use and re-use', in *2003 Dublin Core Conference: Supporting Communities of Discourse and Practice – Metadata Research & Applications*. Seattle, WA: Dublin Core.
38. Ibid.

5

Practical implementation of a metadata strategy

Staffing

Individuals involved in the planning, creation, and maintenance of metadata at a cultural heritage institution must fulfil a variety of roles – many more than one might first imagine. A single individual might fulfil multiple roles, or the roles might be spread across many individuals at a single institution. Exactly who does each individual task can and will be different at each institution; there are no hard and fast rules for who should be involved in metadata work. Rather, seek individuals that thrive on an environment in which there are several different reasonable ways to accomplish a goal, that work well collaboratively, and that aren't afraid to make groundbreaking decisions. These qualities are useful for staff working with metadata issues in any role. Some of the metadata-related roles an institution will likely need are as follows.

Metadata planner

Individuals involved in metadata planning provide a high-level perspective on metadata best practices and how the current project fits into an overall institutional and community infrastructure. They are expert in metadata practice within their community, and are knowledgeable about practices in other communities. These individuals have a keen understanding of similar projects that have been performed at other institutions, and can make recommendations on how decisions from those projects can and should be re-used in the current one. They can provide guidance on when authority control and other advanced metadata features provide benefits worth their cost. These individuals think beyond current systems toward future uses of the metadata being created.

Subject specialist

Subject specialists provide the key link between materials and their metadata. These individuals understand the important features of materials, including expert technical details of various media formats, and ensure these features are adequately represented in the metadata model developed for a project. These individuals have first-hand knowledge of how users interact with these materials, and can often envision expanded uses for them in a digital environment.

User specialist

Individuals knowledgeable about user behaviour in general are essential members of a metadata team. As discussed in previous chapters, metadata creation is best completed with a full understanding of how the metadata will be used, and the user specialist brings this perspective to the table. This individual will provide expert guidance on the types of searching and browsing it will be desirable to support, and will be able to plan studies using various methodologies to get data from actual users to help further refine plans for using metadata for discovery purposes.

Metadata creation

Metadata creators actually produce metadata that conforms to project guidelines. The work of these individuals is best limited to metadata that requires a human to create it, leaving the more routine and objective work to automated methods. Depending on the type of metadata being created, individuals doing this work may need different skills. Many types of metadata can be created by individuals who have a thorough understanding of project guidelines and some understanding of overall project goals, while other types of metadata may require subject expertise in a given knowledge domain or of a given type of media format.

Quality control

It is most effective if the staff performing quality control activities are *not* the same staff that originally created the metadata. Like metadata creators, individuals who perform quality control may or may not need specialised skills, depending on the type of metadata being reviewed.

In any case, these individuals must have a deep understanding of the project metadata creation guidelines, the overall project goals, and how the metadata will be used to provide discovery, delivery, and management functions.

Systems design

Individuals involved in system design for digital projects bring a sense of technical reality to metadata planning discussions. Their expertise regarding existing systems in place at an institution and generic technical mechanisms for implementing new features can help to prioritise the inevitable long list of desired features into a subset that is achievable within project constraints. Knowledge of these same technical mechanisms can also provide new ideas for features to a project team that others might not have envisioned.

Programming

Programming staff implement new tools required by a digital project, or adapt existing ones. These tools might include those for end-user discovery and display, automated metadata creation, manual metadata creation interfaces, quality control, and overall workflow management. These individuals implement the ideas of systems designers and the rest of the metadata planning team.

Once again, it is important to remember that a single individual may serve more than one of these roles on a given project. Good project management will ensure each of these varied perspectives is represented in metadata planning discussions.

What it means to be a metadata specialist

Job titles with the word 'metadata' are increasingly appearing in cultural heritage institutions. Academic libraries were at the forefront of this movement, posting positions for 'metadata specialists' as early as 1995 on the AUTOCAT mailing list.[1] Jobs for metadata specialists quickly expanded beyond academic libraries to other types of institutions, however not necessarily with the term metadata in their title. For example, in 1997, the Minneapolis Institute of Arts posted a job advert for an 'Art Information Access Project Manager'. One of the job functions defined was 'assists in determining and implementing data and metadata standards framework [sic] which support IAIA and AMIGO project goals'.[2] Roles such as 'Metadata librarian', and similar positions, are now common. In January 2007, 24 job postings included the word 'metadata' at the American Library Association JobList site.[3] In July 2004 an email list called 'metadata librarians' was created to bring this community together, 'geared toward discussing qualitative issues central to the metadata and digital library world'.[4]

Yet despite the now-common usage of 'metadata' in job titles and descriptions in cultural heritage institutions, there is little consistency in the duties of the positions or in the skills needed to perform well. In many libraries, a 'metadata librarian' might spend the vast majority of his or her time creating metadata in MARC, and performing associated tasks such as authority control. In others, that same job title might apply to an individual fulfilling the 'metadata planner' role for digital projects. In a museum or archive, a metadata specialist might largely be a content specialist in the area of focus of the organisation. There is an astonishing variety of in-job tasks appearing across job postings for metadata specialists in the cultural heritage area.

The skills required to succeed as a metadata specialist are therefore similarly varied. In-depth knowledge of one or more domains, such as geospatial data, literary texts, or art history might be essential for positions that work in those domains, either in specialised institutions or in specialised departments within larger institutions. A full understanding of the culture, missions, and goals of cultural heritage institutions is useful to make good decisions about how to achieve those goals. Knowledge of the standards relevant to the collections held by the institution is usually essential, as is the ability to quickly learn new standards as they emerge and assess their utility for any given project. Technical aptitude is often important. At the very least, a general understanding of the technology behind how digital resources are created, managed, and delivered to users allows a metadata specialist to be a more knowledgeable member of a project team. Many positions, however, require a much greater level of technical knowledge. Working with XML technologies, including XSLT, is a common job requirement for metadata positions. Technical and structural metadata creation and planning usually requires in-depth knowledge of various file formats. For other positions, more in-depth programming or database design expertise might be required. Excellent writing skills are often valued, for preparing grant proposals, planning documents, metadata creation guidelines, and so on. In short, there is no single core set of skills needed for all metadata-related positions. In the fast-changing digital environment, perhaps the only constant theme among successful individuals in the metadata domain is a commitment to continuously having to learn new approaches and re-evaluate old ones. Flexibility, ingenuity, and excellent problem-solving skills are key.

A metadata specialist, regardless of how many of the roles defined here he might fulfil on a given project, will in most cases also have other responsibilities to the institution as well. In an academic library, a metadata librarian might have professional development, research, or service responsibilities. In any kind of library, a metadata librarian might have reference, bibliographic instruction, or other public service duties. In public libraries and smaller libraries, the metadata specialist might have another job title entirely and take on metadata activities over time in addition to his original responsibilities. In an archive, collections processing might be the responsibility of the individual in charge of metadata activities. In museums, a metadata specialist might have additional exhibition planning responsibilities. In any cultural heritage institution, a metadata specialist might have additional responsibilities for public programming. There are no actual *rules* for what a metadata specialist's job description should include in addition to core metadata expertise. Regardless of how an institution chooses to dole out job responsibilities, metadata specialists should operate as valued and integral members of an institution's professional staff.

Integrating metadata work into a larger infrastructure

An important part of high-level planning for metadata in digital projects is ensuring the work for any given project fits well into an institution's overall technological infrastructure. While digital projects often offer the opportunity to try something new or expand on existing services, the result must be sustainable by your institution. An institutional metadata strategy should be developed with this overarching goal in mind.

Foremost among the factors for integrating individual projects into a technological whole is ensuring consistency among those projects. An inherent tension exists between meeting the specific needs of individual collections and the institutional need for streamlined and consistent workflows. It is unsustainable to build completely new metadata creation and end-use discovery interfaces for every digital collection, but it is equally unacceptable to use exactly the same configuration for every group of materials regardless of format or objectives of the project. A digital library infrastructure, whether a stand-alone digital asset management system, a module of a larger management infrastructure such as an Integrated Library System, a combination of open-source software packages glued together, or entirely locally built, is most effective if it allows easy customisation of the metadata structure for a given collection.

While any given pool of materials will have some unique metadata needs, it is not necessary to start metadata planning from scratch with each successive project. Collection-specific customisation can and should be done in moderation. Build on what you've already done – with good documentation of past decisions, you should be able to review what need to be re-addressed and what can be carried over to the new project with confidence. Carry as many of those decisions over as possible, saving your valuable planning effort for new challenges posed by the current project.

As your institution deals with more and more types of digital materials, it is useful to develop re-usable approaches to metadata for groups of materials – standard methods for dealing with metadata for texts, documentary images, art images, musical recordings, oral histories, moving images, GIS data, biological data, and so on. Each new project adds to an institutional 'toolbox', with systems, documentation, and general approaches that can be re-used for similar materials in the future. Metadata creation systems, storage strategies, and indexing for end-user access can all be informed by past activities. When you do have to design something new, think about how future collections will fit in to the model you are developing.

Integrating into an overall institutional technical infrastructure also involves planning for the short- and long-term storage of metadata. Metadata is an institutional asset, as valuable and critical to operations as the materials to which the metadata applies. The SPECTRUM documentation procedures from the museum community represent one effort to promote treatment of metadata as an institutional asset, describing the need to maintain the 'security of the catalogue'.[5] As metadata is created, it will require secure storage. The nature of metadata creation implies that quick access to existing records for copying or building lists of all terms used in a given field is necessary, requiring the stored metadata to be easily accessible both by humans and by metadata creation systems. Metadata once created will also need to be accessible by end-user search systems and institutional digital asset management systems for reporting, preservation, and other administrative purposes. Full metadata for a digital object, including descriptive, structural, technical, and other types of administrative metadata can grow in size quickly. While metadata for an object in many cases will take up less space than the digital object itself, appropriate planning for the short- and long-term storage and management of that metadata is essential. Metadata storage needs should be taken into account in overall digital repository planning activities.

Methods for sharing and distributing metadata are important components of overall digital library infrastructures. Specific information on sharing metadata appears in Chapters 9, 10 and 11; suffice it to say here that an institutional metadata infrastructure must plan from the beginning to provide this valuable function. For various reasons, you'll likely want to have some level of control over whether and how different types of metadata for different collections are shared. This doesn't mean, however, that preparing metadata for sharing has to be an extra, manual step in your workflow. A robust infrastructure will make it easy to 'turn on' sharing for any given set of metadata as part of the regular project setup process.

Financial implications

Figures on the costs of digitisation for many types of analogue materials are (relatively) well documented,[6-8] although much is still unknown.[9] Costs for metadata creation, by contrast, are not nearly as easy to estimate. It is clear that robust, effective metadata that supports user discovery and collection administration is expensive, yet there are no hard and fast guidelines for exactly *how* expensive metadata creation is. There are a number of reasons for this uncertainty. A primary factor is that the types and extent of metadata created for any two groups of materials may differ widely, making average cost figures a poor indicator of the metadata creation costs for any specific project. Another important factor is the expanded role metadata plays in the digital environment on top of its traditional descriptive role in cultural heritage institutions. New types of metadata for management, preservation, and navigation of digital files add to the total metadata creation costs for a project, on top of more easily predictable costs for descriptive metadata.

Some data exists that can be used as a basis for determining metadata creation costs, however. One report indicates that metadata creation averages 29% of overall project costs.[10] Studies analysing cost factors for library MARC cataloguing,[11-13] might generally be of use for approximating the cost of creating descriptive metadata, but differences in the types of resources being described and the general absence of existing metadata records for these resources for copying can significantly change metadata creation costs from the figures in these studies.

Average cost figures from other institutions can only serve as a general guideline in project planning. To most accurately predict metadata creation costs for a new project at your institution, the best method is to actually perform metadata creation using the tools that will be used in the production environment on a small but representative sample of items from the collection. Be sure to include technical and structural metadata in addition to descriptive metadata in this test. Where this is not possible, use existing cost figures for each type of metadata created from projects as similar as possible to yours. Tools such as the RLG Worksheet for Estimating Digital Reformatting Costs[14] can be used to help perform the necessary calculations to estimate costs for an entire project, but only after reasonable per-item and per-hour estimates are developed. In any case, be prepared for initial estimates to be either higher or lower than expected, and be ready to adjust accordingly.

In addition to metadata creation costs, creating and maintaining metadata for digital collections introduces additional roles into an institution's base budget. Metadata specialists, programmers and the other roles described at the beginning of this chapter are all needed, even past the initial metadata creation phase. In some cases, repurposing of existing staff can be done to meet these needs. Library cataloguers or those with collection processing responsibilities often possess the basic skills needed to select metadata formats, write metadata creation guidelines or create descriptive or other types of metadata, when given appropriate training. Many cultural heritage institutions already employ programmers to run catalogues, websites, and other systems.

Grants can be an effective means of adding new staff at key points in the development of institutional digital infrastructure. However, grants also require significant commitment on the part of base-funded staff to plan projects, to hire, train and supervise grant-funded staff, and sustain the initiative once grant funding runs out. Exclusively using grant-funded staff for digital initiatives is unsustainable over the long-term; institutions must find ways to build digital collections expertise in permanent staff as well. Use grants as kick-start methods, not as the only means to complete a digital project.

Regardless of the staffing model chosen, working with digital collections generally significantly adds to the total workload of a cultural heritage institution. Digital projects can bring valuable exposure to an institution, meet expanded patron needs, and build technological infrastructure. But these benefits come at a price – significant institutional commitment must be made to build and sustain digital collections. Each institution must find its own balance between the use of grants, permanent specialised staff, and more generalised staff.

All staff involved in digital projects will require an institutional investment in ongoing professional development. Digital library technology is evolving at an astonishing pace. The oft-cited Moore's Law predicts the number of transistors on a circuit doubles 'about every two years',[15] resulting in exponential growth in processing power – although the exact nature of the 'law' and the effectiveness of its predictions have been questioned.[16] Similar enormous growth rates have been reported for hard disk space, from 5 megabytes (MB) in 1956, to standard desktop computer hard drives of 80 to 500 gigabytes (GB) in 2006, with terabyte-sized drives available for the average consumer in early 2007.[17] Programming languages are created, merged with others, and go out of fashion.[18] New Web browsers are frequently being released, resulting in the 'hot' browser changing frequently over time, from Mosaic in the early days of the Web to Netscape to Internet Explorer to Firefox and beyond. Best practices for file formats used to store digital objects are similarly changing over time.[19] For example, for still images the trend has moved from PhotoCD in the early days of digital libraries,[20] to TIFF shortly thereafter,[21] to investigations of the suitability of JPEG2000 and other wavelet-based formats in the first decade of the twenty-first century.[22] For other types of resources, such as moving images, no clear best practice exists yet for the choice of a master file format for long-term use. Lack of planning for these technological changes can result in loss or obsolescence of data, undermining the hard work and expense that has gone into creating that data in the first place. A 2006 report by the UK-based Digital Preservation Coalition reported 'Only 29% of respondents in the 2005 DPC survey could say they have not lost access to some digital information, as a result of it being impossible or too expensive to recover. Even when referring to their most important type of data, this proportion only rose to 43%'.[23]

To ensure digital objects created can be preserved, and to meet constantly-changing user needs, staff involved at any level in a digital project will need institutional support for keeping up with new developments, attending conferences to learn about the state of the art in their area of specialisation, and obtaining formal training in new technologies that improve the ways digital collections can be created and delivered. This type of professional development isn't a 'perk' in this field – it's an essential part of the cost of developing and maintaining digital collections. The expense of ongoing professional development is easy to forget when planning digital projects, yet it is a key part of ensuring digital resources can be sustained over time.

Notes

1. McClellan, G. (1995) 'Job Posting: Metadata Specialist', *AUTOCAT: Library cataloging and authorities discussion group* (AUTOCAT@UBVM. CC.BUFFALO.EDU), 30 November 1995, 14:30:56–0600.
2. Sayre, S. (1997) 'Job Opp: Internet Database Proj. Manager', *Museum-L mailing list* (MUSEUM-L@home.ease.lsoft.com), 18 November 1997, 23:52:38 +0000. Available at *http://home.ease.lsoft.com/scripts/wa.exe? A2=ind9711C&L=MUSEUM-L&P=R3564*.
3. American Library Association. 'ALA Joblist', available at *http://joblist .ala.org*.
4. Metadata Librarians Listserv (*http://metadatalibrarians.monarchos.com*).
5. MDA. 'The development of the SPECTRUM standard', available at *http://www.mda.org.uk/specdev.htm*.
6. Puglia, S. (1999) 'The costs of digital imaging projects', *RLG DigiNews*, 3(5): available at *http://www.rlg.org/preserv/diginews/diginews3-5.html# feature*.
7. HEDS (2002) 'Matrix of potential cost factors', available at *http://heds .herts.ac.uk/resources/matrix.html*.
8. University of Michigan Digital Library Services (2001) 'Assessing the costs of conversion: Making of America IV: The American Voice 1850–1876'. Ann Arbor, MI: University of Michigan; available at *http://www.umdl .umich.edu/pubs/moa4_costs.pdf*.
9. Hughes, L. (ed) (2003) 'The price of digitization: new cost models for cultural and educational institutions', in *NINCH Symposium Report*. New York, NY: New York Public Library.
10. Puglia, S. (1999) 'The costs of digital imaging projects', *RLG DigiNews*, 3(5): available at *http://www.rlg.org/preserv/diginews/diginews3-5.html#feature*.
11. Morris, D.E., Hobert, C.B., Osmus, L. and Wool, G. (2000) 'Cataloging staff costs revisited', *Library Resources & Technical Services*, 44(2): 70–83.
12. Harris, G. (1989) 'Historic cataloging costs, issues, and trends', *The Library Quarterly*, 59(1): 1–21.
13. Hurlbert, T. and Dujmic, L.L. (2004) 'Factors affecting cataloging time: an in-house survey', *Technical Services Quarterly*, 22(2): 1–14.

14. Research Libraries Group (1997) 'RLG Worksheet for estimating digital reformatting costs', available at *http://www.rlg.org/en/pdfs/RLGWorksheet.pdf*.

15. Moore, G.E. (1965) 'Cramming more components onto integrated circuits', *Electronics*, 38(8): 114–17. Available at *http://download.intel.com/research/silicon/moorespaper.pdf*.

16. Tuomi, I. (2002) 'The lives and death of Moore's Law', *First Monday*, 7(11): available at *http://www.firstmonday.org/issues/issue7_11/tuomi/*.

17. Goldsborough, R. (2006) 'The past and future of hard drives', *Information Today*, 23(10): 37–9.

18. A graphical representation of the history of programming languages can be found at *http://www.oreilly.com/pub/a/oreilly/news/languageposter_0504.html*.

19. For information on file formats, see: Library of Congress. 'Sustainability of digital formats planning for Library of Congress collections format description categories', available at *http://www.digitalpreservation.gov/formats/fdd/browse_list.shtml*.

20. Kenney, A.R. and Rieger, O.Y. (1998) 'Using Kodak Photo CD technology for preservation and access: a guide for librarians, archivists, and curators', *RLG DigiNews*, 2(3): available at *http://www.rlg.org/preserv/diginews/diginews23.html#feature*.

21. Digital Library Federation Benchmark Working Group (2002) 'Benchmark for faithful digital reproductions of monographs and serials. Version 1', available at *http://purl.oclc.org/DLF/benchrepro0212*.

22. Janosky, J.S. and Witthus, R.W. (2004) 'Using JPEG2000 for enhanced preservation and web access of digital archives – a case study', in *IS&T's 2004 Archiving Conference*. San Antonio, TX: IST; pp. 145–9. Available at *http://charlesolson.uconn.edu/Works_in_the_Collection/Melville_Project/IST_Paper3.pdf*.

23. Waller, M. and Sharpe, R. (2006) 'Mind the gap: assessing digital preservation needs in the UK'. York, UK: Digital Preservation Coalition; available at *http://www.dpconline.org/docs/reports/uknamindthegap.pdf*.

Part III
Systems design

An institution's metadata creation strategy must be tied heavily to the applications and systems that will use the metadata records. In certain cases, a system may be conceived after the digital resources and their metadata were created. In those cases, a balance must be found between adapting the system design to take into account the existing metadata, and re-purposing and adapting the metadata to the new application. There must always be a good match between the metadata that exists and the system functions provided. However, when metadata does not yet exist, it is possible to define a metadata creation policy according to the system that will be designed. This is the preferable option, as it makes the match between the two more complete.

In all cases, users should be at the centre of the system design process. Although this may seem obvious, the motivations for setting up a digital project are complex, and a user-centred focus is easy to lose. Including a user specialist on a project team and working towards clearly-defined target audiences are common ways of maintaining this focus. Many different methodologies can be used at different stages of a project to assess user needs. Whatever strategies are used, the design of metadata records must match the expected functions of a system.

Part III of this book focuses on the factors that must be taken into consideration during the system design stage. Chapter 6 describes the typical functions implemented in a digital library system, their evolution, and the way in which the metadata interacts with the system to enable those functions. Chapter 7 analyses the user interfaces that can be built to take advantage of metadata for information discovery.

6

Functions performed by a digital library system

A digital library system can be described as a set of tools that make digital resources and their metadata available. Whereas the term 'digital library' might suggest that brick and mortar libraries have simply migrated to the Web and merely added digital resources to online catalogues, this evolution is actually far more complex. The term 'digital libraries' can mean many different things, from a simpler 'libraries putting collections online' perspective, to a more expansive definition encompassing materials held by many different types of cultural heritage institutions, to one referring to a thematic collection of material compiled outside of a traditional 'library', such as the ACM Digital Library,[1] which pulls together professional publications of the Association for Computing Machinery. The meaning of the term 'digital library' has been discussed in many forums, including at the European Conference on Digital Libraries 2003 by a panel of actors involved in digital library development, chaired by Stefan Gradmann.[2] A significant point raised by that panel was that by calling a digital library an application that makes available digital resources from cultural heritage institutions, one introduces a bias towards functions traditionally fulfilled by those institutions, preferencing these functions over others. Whereas access and retrieval of information is a core component of digital libraries, they often also perform a number of other functions, including providing context for resources, facilitating the creation of virtual exhibitions, assisting with the management of digital objects, and supporting the digital preservation process.

User expectations for digital library systems are expanding with constant advances in the online world. Often, inspiration for new services can come from outside the cultural heritage sector. The California Digital Library, inspired by Amazon.com,[3] has experimented with a recommendation system that takes advantage of information on user behaviours.[4] The University of Pennsylvania Libraries[5] have implemented a system called PennTags to help their users manage Web resources together with citations from Library systems, borrowing from the success of user tagging systems such as Flickr[6] and del.icio.us.[7] More traditional library catalogues interfaces are expanding functionality as well. The implementation of commercial search technology from Endeca[8] on top of a traditional Integrated Library System at North Carolina State University[9,10] has demonstrated in a concrete way some of the potential for new features using existing data structures in libraries. No single text can cover the myriad of interesting features available in online systems at any given time. This chapter will focus on the abstract, core functions of digital library systems of which the previous examples were specific implementations, while the following chapter will cover how metadata helps achieve those core functions.

The user at the centre of the system design

A digital library system should be designed for its users. These users include not only what are typically thought of as 'end-users' (our patrons, researchers, visitors, or customers), but also our professional institutional staff. Users can be specialists in an area, or a novice. A human user might be hearing or visually impaired, and therefore access digital resources with specialised software and/or devices. Users will likely come from a variety of technological environments, including high-end workstations and extremely old models with limited bandwidth, processing power and software. Other software applications can also be users of digital library systems, sharing metadata and/or content between systems.

The first steps in building a system involve defining who the current and potential users are, and deciding which of these groups will be actively supported. Your institution may have a mandate to serve specific groups of users, for example, citizens of a given geographical region, students at a University, or users with certain types of disabilities. It is not always possible to anticipate who all the users of a system that does not yet exist are going to be. However, it is possible to define groups of target users, what the system must do for them, and begin to think about how the system can best perform the defined tasks. These definitions are most useful if they are fairly specific. Stating 'my target users are students' and 'they must be able to retrieve scholarly literature in economics' is not enough. The analysis should include what the target users *cannot* do at this point, for example if a similar service does not exist, or one that does exist lacks key functionality. This analysis of users and their needs then allows specific system functions that support those needs to be defined, such as what types of search indexes are needed and what result-sorting options should be included, as discussed in the next chapter.

A variety of methods exist for gathering data on users, including heuristic evaluation, focus groups, surveys, contextual inquiry, log analysis, card sorts, paper prototype walkthroughs, and task scenarios.[11] Current and potential users, collection managers, subject specialists, and technical staff can all contribute to a definition of functions to be implemented in a digital library system. Both the systems creators and the users have a role in inventing new technological services and products. New ideas can come from either side, and the other can then confirm the usefulness and feasibility of the idea. New models can emerge from users that had not been originally imagined by system designers.[12] Technology enthusiasts and early adopters willing to test technologies that have not yet matured help ideas become real products.[13]

Most systems, however, will implement functions that have already been implemented and tested in other places, with other content. When designing your own system, a general review of systems at similar institutions with similar content can help define your own requirements. For example, search functionality can vary from one digital library system to another. A review of several systems can demonstrate various options to potential users, and help focus their feedback into specific recommendations the system designers can use. In addition to actual user studies, there is a great deal to be learned from published literature in the area. For example, studies have been published on search behaviours in library catalogues,[14] in digital libraries,[15] with EAD finding aids[16] and with specific types of material such as digital images,[17] among countless others. Experts in designing and interpreting the data from user studies are essential if their results are to be meaningful.[18]

Digital library system functions

User discovery and delivery

As noted above, the most visible and discussed function of a digital library system is to provide discovery and delivery services for end-users. Elaine Svenonius provides a history of the development of the functions of a bibliographic record, beginning this discussion with a reminder that 'The first step in designing a bibliographic system is to state its objectives'.[19] There is a necessary dependency between the metadata records in a system and the functions that system can provide.

Although the state of the art related to the specifics of discovery and delivery functions is constantly changing, the International Federation of Library Associations and Institutions (IFLA) 1998 report, *Functional Requirements for Bibliographic Records* (FRBR) has defined a set of 'uses that are made of bibliographic data':

> to **find** entities that correspond to the user's stated search criteria (i.e., to locate either a single entity or a set of entities in a file or database as the result of a search using an attribute or relationship of the entity);
>
> to **identify** an entity (i.e., to confirm that the entity described corresponds to the entity sought, or to distinguish between two or more entities with similar characteristics);
>
> to **select** an entity that is appropriate to the user's needs (i.e., to choose an entity that meets the user's requirements with respect to content, physical format, etc., or to reject an entity as being inappropriate to the user's needs);
>
> to acquire or **obtain** access to the entity described (i.e., to acquire an entity through purchase, loan, etc., or to access an entity electronically through an online connection to a remote computer).[20]

While the FRBR user tasks were conceived primarily for the data present in library catalogues, the framework is useful for digital library systems as well. The grouping of specific tasks into this larger conceptual framework has generated a great deal of discussion, with additional tasks such as 'navigate' and 'relate' suggested but ultimately considered to be contained within the original four user tasks by the IFLA FRBR Review Group.[21] One can imagine additional (or perhaps more specific) tasks of a digital library system supporting the *use* of an object once discovered, including:

- grouping objects in subcategories or collections;
- interpreting an object by providing documentation, provenance information and potentially an analysis of the object;
- sharing an object between systems or with other users.

With the development of digital library applications, and the implementation of digital library systems not only in libraries but also in the commercial sector, in archives, in museums, in learning management platforms and countless other environments, discovery and use functions of these systems continue to expand, and more traditional functions are re-imagined in new ways. Each technical function of a digital library system, for example, *retrieving* items, should be designed to fulfil a defined user task, for example, *find*. This technical function of the system is likely to be made up of a number of steps on the back end: for example, parsing a query, sending it to appropriate indexes, then ordering and displaying the results. Planning for a digital library system involves first defining the conceptual user tasks supported, identifying the functions a system will provide to achieve those tasks, then developing the specific technical means for achieving those functions.

Digital object management

While the discovery and delivery functions of a digital library system typically receive the most attention, the nuts and bolts of managing digital objects is a key function of digital library systems. In some sense, this is the 'magic' behind the system – the functions that, when they are working, are invisible to end-users and many content managers as well.

'Publishing' digital collections is a prime example of this phenomenon. The development of a digital library collection is a complex process, involving many steps that may happen over a long period of time. A robust digital library system will have methods for managing content before it is made public – if it does this in too simplistic a way, the system becomes a hindrance rather than a help. Maintaining a configurable set of record statuses as administrative metadata is one part of managing content relative to its public availability. An institution might need, for example, record statuses to indicate that a digital object exists but not its descriptive metadata, that descriptive metadata exists but not a digital object, that a master digital object exists but delivery versions have not yet been generated, that basic descriptive metadata exists but needs review or enhancement, and so on. Each of these statuses would control who can view or edit an object, and drive 'task lists' for various project staff. As more and more cultural heritage institutions move away from a 'project'-based approach (where a finite group of content and metadata is created in a relatively short period of time, then the collection is made public all at once and changed very little after that) to a 'program'-based approach (where collections grow and change over time, with ongoing additions of content), this sort of functionality becomes even more essential.

The keeping of statistics is another essential 'behind the scenes' function of a digital library system. Statistics on both end-user behaviour and on administrative functions are necessary. The ability to easily generate reports indicating which collections and items are most heavily used (and which are not), the ratio of the use of online-viewable to downloadable versions of objects, and so on, can all help inform the design of functionality improvements and the selection of new collections for delivery. Search logs are useful for evaluating how effective existing descriptive metadata and the discovery system are at meeting user needs, and to inform on the types of content users are looking for in the system. Reports listing zero-hit searches are especially effective in locating gaps between user expectations and system performance. Statistics on administrative functions such as production rates of digitising and metadata creation staff, how many times and in what ways descriptive metadata records are updated over time, how often any given vocabulary or specific term is used in a descriptive metadata record, and so on, are all useful for project management, quality control, and reporting purposes.

Many other administrative functions are also possible for digital library systems. Maintaining relationships between different versions of the same digital object, for example a book as a fully-marked up TEI file, a plain-text ASCII file, a PDF for downloading and printing and raster page images at three sizes, must be managed by the system and the appropriate version rendered for the end-user at the appropriate time. A system may need to use rights metadata for access control in cases where usage must be restricted, or record object transactions for royalty payment purposes. A digital library system might include functions to support a quality review process for digitisation or metadata creation, selecting random objects for review, performing automated quality checks, and recording the results of these actions. There is no single agreed-upon set of administrative actions all digital library systems must fulfil; each software package comes with a different supported set. A key part of selecting a digital library system is to define the administrative functions needed in your institution and to use those defined functions as part of your selection criteria.

Preservation

Preservation of digital objects and their metadata is another essential function of a digital library system. Given the large amount of time and money involved in creating and providing access to digital content, and the almost endless amount of worthy content out there that may never become a priority for delivery via a managed digital library system, cultural heritage institutions simply cannot afford not to keep the content and metadata they do create safe and relevant over the long term. True digital preservation is not an easy task, however, and the cultural heritage community is just beginning to explore what it truly means to 'preserve' a digital object and its attendant metadata. The most comprehensive look at this question in the cultural heritage community to date comes from a group jointly sponsored by OCLC and RLG entitled PREMIS (PREservation Metadata Implementation Strategies).[22] The PREMIS group released a final report in May of 2005 which defines a data model of entities involved in digital preservation activities, a data dictionary of semantic units of data related to the entities in the data model, and examples of metadata useful for preservation of several types of digital objects.[23] The PREMIS group defines digital preservation as a dynamic, ongoing activity, and preservation metadata as 'the information a repository uses to support the digital preservation process'.

Initiatives such as PREMIS, however, can only define functions and metadata that help implement a digital preservation policy. They cannot *set* a digital preservation policy for an institution. High-level decisions on what types of content an institution wishes to commit to preserving, to what degree (save the components as they were originally created, migrate to new formats in the future, etc.), and what sorts of ongoing checks are needed to feel confident in the safety of a digital object define what sorts of digital preservation functions a digital library system should provide. Like any kind of metadata, preservation metadata is best created and stored first by clearly defining the functions it will support and only then delving into the details of the data needed to provide that functionality.

As the state of the art in digital preservation is changing rapidly, it is difficult for production systems to keep up with the functionality the current thinking in the area suggests. Cultural heritage professionals are best served at this time by keeping up with new developments in the digital preservation arena, monitoring the metadata stored in digital library systems in relation to defined digital preservation functions, and lobbying system designers to support digital preservation functions as they are more fully defined and included in institutional preservation policies. Ongoing attention to these topics is an essential part of the overall digital preservation process.

Identifying and supporting the functions of unfamiliar systems

Even with the best planning, it is not possible to anticipate all the functions of systems that metadata may need to support into the future. Systems change over time, new functions are implemented, some of which may not even be conceived of today. Even in the short term, metadata will likely be shared with other applications, perhaps even outside of the cultural heritage sector, that have different capabilities than the system for which the metadata was originally developed. Some systems may focus solely on user discovery, and others perhaps on the preservation of digital objects or intellectual property management. These current and future systems are likely to be increasingly interconnected.

No single strategy exists for ensuring metadata is usable for the functioning of an unknown system. The use of documented standards and best practices for metadata structure, metadata content, and vocabularies as described in Part II of this book represent a good start towards this lofty goal. When metadata conforms to a set of documented expectations, any new system is more likely to be able to interpret and use it effectively. More on what makes metadata 'shareable' can be found in Chapter 11.

It is often the case that one may know a specific system that metadata will be used in, but not to know precisely how that system uses metadata to perform its defined functions. This is typically the case in union catalogues and in distributed systems such as those built with the Open Archives Protocol for Metadata Harvesting. The union catalogue or metadata aggregator may have some published guidelines, but these rarely explain in detail how specific metadata elements are being used. A creative approach to this problem comes from Bill Moen, who has experimented with what he calls 'radioactive records'.[24] These records were specifically constructed to use distinctive values that would not normally be encountered in the target systems. Once the radioactive record is in the system, the metadata provider can then analyse where the distinctive values appear in search indexes, displays, and so on. The metadata provider could then determine if changes were needed to ensure, for example, a particular metadata element gets included in a subject index or appears in a short record display.

Metadata for a purpose

While general guidance on good metadata practice exists, and is discussed elsewhere in this book, there is no one set of hard and fast rules by which all metadata creation should abide. Defined user tasks and system functions will always drive what sort of metadata is created and how it is structured. Karen Coyle provides a succinct summary of this idea:

> Metadata is ...
>
> ... *constructed* ... (Metadata is wholly artificial, created by human beings.)
>
> ... *for a purpose* ... (There is no universal metadata. For metadata to be useful it has to serve a purpose.)
>
> ... *to facilitate an activity* ... (There's something that you **do** with metadata.)[25]

There is no monolithic, one-size-fits-all metadata record. All metadata formats, from MARC to Dublin Core to ONIX and far beyond, are designed with a particular set of system functions and a particular set of uses in mind. None can function as the single source of metadata for all possible applications on its own. Recognising the assumptions underlying any metadata format, standard, or best practice is a key part of ensuring the metadata created as part of a digital project is usable by systems. Carefully consider whether all metadata being created meets a defined function of the system. It is a waste of resources to create metadata that isn't used, either today or in reasonably-imagined other current or future systems. Don't be afraid to think big in terms of what kind of functionality your system can provide; however, do avoid simply using a field from a metadata structure standard just because it's there. Think beyond your local system for functions to support, but always know what purpose any given metadata element is expected to fulfil.

Once desired system functions have been determined, work can begin to ensure metadata is created that can drive those functions. The metadata design and creation processes in place must provide accurate and usable information to the application envisioned. Minimum metadata elements for indexing and display can be defined based on user and system expectations for these functions. More advanced functions will likely place other requirements on metadata as well. For example, if the system is to provide sorting of search results by date, then a date in a machine-readable form such as '1896-10-16' is necessary, or the system must have the capability of translating date formats such as 'Oct 16th, 1896' or '1896?' or 'Autumn 1896' into a form that can be used for machine sorting. If the system is to provide sorting by names in alphabetical order, the system must know what part of a name to sort on. This could be performed by recording parts of names in separate fields, using consistent separators between parts of names such as commas, or by storing names directly as sortable strings. Which of these and other options is appropriate for any given application depends on the other functions the system will need to perform on those names.

While it's not possible to create metadata that can fulfil *all possible* purposes, it is frequently the case that any given piece of metadata can serve at least more than one purpose. This is often accomplished by the system processing a piece of metadata in a pre-defined way to generate a different view of the same data for a different purpose. For example, an ISO 639-2 code[26] is a commonly-used encoding for a machine-readable representation of the language of a resource, which is useful for browsing resources by language or limiting search results. However, displaying 'gle' to a user to indicate the Irish language is certainly not ideal. In this case, it may be reasonable to store the language metadata in the system according to the ISO 639-2 standard. The system could then perform a 'decoding' task from the ISO codes to their human readable equivalents. This same decoding task could be performed when translating metadata from an internal system format into a different format useful for sharing, as described in Chapter 10.

In some cases, where system functions have contrary requirements, it is not possible to provide lossless machine translation from one version of a piece of metadata to another fulfilling a different function. System designers may choose to reconcile these requirements, to choose one function as a priority, say, consistent indexing takes priority over a user-friendly display. Another, more time-consuming, option is to repeat the same information in different forms to support the multiple functions. The Cataloging Cultural Objects (CCO) content standard distinguishes data used for indexing from that used for the display (see Box 6.1), under the assumption that creating user-friendly display strings for complex data such as the artistic medium is outside the capabilities of the vast majority of currently-available systems.[27] The system function defined, the user need driving this function, the metadata standards involved and the system capabilities are all factors in deciding how to deal with multiple requirements for a single piece of data.

| Box 6.1 | CCO-style values for display and machine-readability encoded in VRA Core 4.0[28] |

```
<materialSet>
    <display>oil paint on canvas</display>
    <material type="medium" vocab="AAT"refid=
    "300015050">oil paint</material>
    <material type="support" vocab="AAT"refid=
    "300014078">canvas</material>
</materialSet>
```

The inter-relatedness of system functionality, metadata standards, and user needs can present a complex challenge to those designing digital library projects. Chapter 7 will discuss ways of making practical decisions, weighing each of these factors, about how to use metadata to support defined system functions for discovery.

Notes

1. Association for Computing Machinery. 'The ACM Digital Library', available at *http://portal.acm.org/dl.cfm*.
2. ECDL (2003) *7th European Conference on Research and Advanced Technology for Digital Libraries*, available at *http://www.ecdl2003.org/*. See also Gradmann, S. (2003) 'How digital will libraries ever be? Musings on the limits of a popular metaphor', in *Informacné Správanie a Digitálne Kniznice* (Information Behaviour in Digital Libraries). Bratislava: Ikaros; pp. 27–40.
3. Amazon (*http://www.amazon.com*)
4. See Whitney, C. and Schifft, L. (2006) 'The Melvyl recommender project: developing library recommendation services', *D-Lib Magazine*, 12(12): available at *http://www.dlib.org/dlib/december06/whitney/12whitney.html*.
5. University of Pennsylvania, PennTags (*http://tags.library.upenn.edu/*).
6. Flickr (*http://www.flickr.com*).
7. Del.icio.us (*http://del.icio.us/*).
8. Endeca (*http://www.endeca.com/*).
9. North Carolina State University, NCSU Libraries Catalog (*http://www.lib.ncsu.edu/catalog/*).
10. Antelman, K., Lynema, E. and Pace, A.K. (2006) 'Toward a 21st century library catalog', *Information Technology and Libraries*, 25(3): 128–39. Available at *http://eprints.rclis.org/archive/00007332/*.

11. For more information on usability studies in the library environment, see Covey, D.T. (2002) *Usage and Usability Assessment: Library Practices and Concerns*. Washington, DC: Digital Library Federation and Council on Library and Information Resources; available at *http://www.clir.org/PUBS/reports/pub105/contents.html*. See also Campbell, N. (ed) (2001) *Usability Assessment of Library-Related Web Sites*. Chicago, IL: LITA and Lehman, T. and Nikkel, T. (eds) (2007) *Making Library Web Sites Usable*. New York: Neal-Schuman.

12. On technology development by lead users, see Von Hippel, E. (1986) 'Lead users: a source of novel product concepts', *Management Science*, 32(7): 791–805.

13. See for example Moore, G.A. (2002) *Crossing the Chasm: Marketing and Selling High-Tech Products to Mainstream Customers*. Revised edn. New York: HarperCollins.

14. For example: Yu, H. and Young, M.(2004) 'The impact of Web search engines on subject searching in OPAC', *Information Technology and Libraries*, 23(4): 168–80.

15. Assadi, H., Beauvisage, T., Lupovici, C. and Cloarec, T. (2003) 'Users and uses of online digital libraries in France', in Koch, T. and Solvberg, I. (eds) *Proceedings of the 7th European Conference on Research and Advanced Technology for Digital Libraries, Trondheim, Norway, 17–22 August 2003*. Heidelberg: Springer Lecture Notes in Computer Science 2769; pp. 1–12.

16. See for example: Sexton, A., Turner, C., Yeo, G. and Hockey, S. (2004) 'Understanding users: a prerequisite for developing new technologies', *Journal of the Society of Archivists*, 25(1): 33–49; doi:10.1080/003798104 2000199133.

17. See for example: Dalmau, M. (2003) 'Charles W. Cushman photograph collection: report on the group and individual walkthrough', available at *http://www.letrs.indiana.edu/~mdalmau/cushman/prototype/designDocs/cushWalkFinalReport.pdf*.

18. See for example: Dumas, J.S. and Redish, J.C. (1999) *A Practical Guide to Usability Testing*. Bristol, UK: Intellect Ltd.

19. Svenonius, E. (2001) *The Intellectual Foundation of Information Organization*. Cambridge, MA: MIT Press; p. 15

20. International Federation of Library Associations (1998) 'Functional requirements for bibliographic records', in *IFLA Section on Cataloguing*. München: K.G. Saur; p. 82. Available at *http://www.ifla.org/VII/s13/frbr/frbr.pdf*.

21. IFLA (2005) 'Minutes of the FRBR Review Group's Meeting', Oslo, 18 August 2005. Available at *http://www.ifla.org/VII/s13/wgfrbr/FRBRRG_MeetingReport_20050818.pdf*.

22. OCLC. 'PREMIS (PREservation Metadata: Implementation Strategies) Working Group', available at *http://www.oclc.org/research/projects/pmwg/*.

23. OCLC and RLG (2005) 'PREMIS Working Group: Data Dictionary for Preservation Metadata', available at *http://www.oclc.org/research/projects/pmwg/premis-final.pdf*.

24. Moen, W.E., Hammer, S., Taylor, M., Thomale, J. and Yoon, J.-W. (2005) 'An extensible approach to interoperability testing: the use of special diagnostic

records in the context of Z39.50 and online library catalogs', in *Proceedings of the American Society for Information Science and Technology*, 42(1): available at *http://dx.doi.org/10.1002/meet.14504201196*.

25. Coyle, K. (2004) 'Metadata: data with a purpose. A brief introduction to metadata, especially for librarians', available at *http://www.kcoyle.net/meta_purpose.html*.

26. See Library of Congress. 'Codes for the representation of names of languages', available at *http://www.loc.gov/standards/iso639-2/*.

27. Baca, M. (2006) *Cataloging Cultural Objects: A Guide to Describing Cultural Works and Their Images*. Chicago, IL: American Library Association.

28. Visual Resources Association (2007) 'VRA Core 4.0 Element Description', available at *http://www.vraweb.org/projects/vracore4/*.

7

Metadata that drives discovery functionality

Despite the many distinct functions of digital library systems, discovery functionality remains a primary focus for most projects. Defining how this discovery functionality – search, browse, more advanced discovery functions, and the display of results – should operate is a key part of planning a digital library project. As described in Chapter 6, the relationship between the structure and content of metadata, specific system functions, and user expectations is a close one. This chapter details the discovery-related tasks performed by many systems and provides practical advice on ways implementers might choose to design discovery functions.

The role of user studies

Understanding user expectations is the first and most important step in designing the discovery functionality for a digital library system. User studies are useful tools for understanding these expectations, as described in Chapter 6. While users are (often frustratingly) diverse in their information needs and discovery preferences, user studies can demonstrate general trends in user preferences, and this information can be used to design systems that give interfaces to meet most needs quickly and easily, yet offer additional options for those that need them.

While user studies can be performed after metadata is created, the relationship of metadata to discovery capability is so close that it is generally desirable to perform user studies prior to choosing metadata standards and writing metadata creation guidelines. Planning for discovery capability is best performed *before* metadata is created. User studies can inform many different aspects of system design, including which data elements are most important to users for searching and browsing, which vocabularies best match users' language, and what sorts of results processing features are most needed in a given system. Studies can be as simple as a small focus group, or be conceived as a formal research agenda. An example of the latter can be seen in the planning for an online sheet music project by the Indiana University Digital Library Program. This project team performed a progressive series of user studies, including query logs analysis, a card sort activity, a task scenario study, and an email content analysis. The results from this series of studies drove decisions about what metadata model to use for the project, what controlled vocabularies to use for certain fields, the format of values for certain fields, on which field to best focus cataloguing efforts, and which metadata elements to focus on for the search and browse system.[1] The *Minnesota Bridges: Minnesota's Gateway to Environmental Information* project conducted similar studies 'to develop a description of 'what people want to know' about Minnesota's environment and natural resources'.[2]

The scope and formality of user studies needed for effective systems design will be different for every institution and for every project. An institution might consider the project budget, project timeline, existing data on users and their behaviours, and the scope and visibility of the digital library system as factors in determining how much time and effort to spend on user studies. It is better to do user studies on a small scale than to rely on systems and content expertise alone to make decisions about the design of a discovery system.

Analysing metadata for planning systems

While it is important to consider discovery functionality in depth before creating metadata, there are usually details of a discovery system that cannot be finalised until a significant amount of metadata creation has been performed. This metadata analysis step will take into consideration the characteristics of metadata brought in from elsewhere over which an institution has little or no control, differences between characteristics of metadata actually created in-house versus pre-project expectations, and the diversity of materials in a system when different metadata models are in use. For each of the decisions regarding discovery functionality described later in this chapter, some or all of the following criteria should be considered.

Metadata quality

While good quality metadata is generally a goal for digital library projects, there are many reasons the quality of metadata for any given group of resources might not be as high as one would like. Design discovery capabilities to act upon metadata as it *should* exist in a system based on project expectations for metadata quality, whatever they might be. While no system can overcome all simple errors in metadata records, understanding how a given pool of metadata meets other quality factors such as conformance to expectations, logical consistency and coherence, timeliness, and accessibility, as described in Chapter 4, will help define what sorts of discovery features a system needs to implement in order to provide meaningful results to end-users.

Level of detail

More detailed metadata records in a system and more granular individual metadata values allow for more precise discovery. In a homogeneous system that contains only one type of material, specific discovery capabilities tailored towards that type of material will be possible. In a more heterogeneous system, or one with sparser metadata records, it may only be possible to implement more general discovery features.

Presence and absence of metadata values

Just because a field exists in a metadata record doesn't mean it contains a meaningful value. While some fields may be required by a metadata format or by local metadata creation policy, most will not be, but will rather be completed only when a value is known, applicable, and valuable. Often, the percentage of records within a whole that make use of a given field will not be predictable before metadata creation occurs. It is only after metadata exists that an analysis of whether enough records contain a particular metadata element to be useful as a search or browse target is possible. If only a small proportion (there is no hard and fast rule for what 'small' is in this case) of records in a system use a particular element, the utility of this element as a search or browse index on its own is greatly diminished. In this case, including this element as a separate indexed field could actually reduce the usefulness of a discovery system.

Consistency of metadata values

Metadata elements that use controlled terminology such as name authority lists, subject thesauri, or smaller vocabularies for features such as content type are likely to be more useful as search limits, browsing categories, links to execute new searches from a results display and results grouping options than elements with less consistent values. Elements with less consistent values, such as descriptive and free-text fields are more likely to be useful only as search indexes.

Uniqueness of metadata values

Metadata elements that have the same value across all or a large proportion of records in a system are unlikely to be useful for display to users, especially in a brief record display where the goal is to provide the user with information needed to distinguish one resource from another. They are also unlikely to be useful as search indexes or browse categories, as any value will either retrieve all records or none. These elements are more useful in aggregated environments, when these records are combined with others that have different values for the element.

Relationships between metadata values

Many metadata elements can contain values that have a conceptual relationship to one another. For example, a topical term from a controlled vocabulary might have hierarchical relationships to broader and narrower terms, a personal name might represent an individual with a familial or professional relationship to other individuals that might be of interest to a searcher, or a specific content type might be an instance of a more general type. These relationships are not generally recorded in metadata instance records; therefore, to make use of them to improve retrieval the system must know about these relationships and act upon them. This is typically accomplished through the use of controlled vocabularies and authority files.

Machine readability of metadata values

Values that are stored in machine-readable form are more easily used as search limits and results grouping and sorting options than those that are not. They are also more likely to need translation into a human-readable form for display and require some sort of query parsing to be used in a search index, as discussed in Chapter 6.

Searching

Keyword indexes

The predominance of Google and its counterparts in online discovery services at this time has created a strong user expectation towards an initial search screen consisting of a single box in which to enter a query of any length, and a button to start the search. For many types of resource that might be included in digital library systems, this model is appropriate for a simple search page.

The challenge in this case is determining which fields from stored metadata should be indexed in this simple search box. Normally, only those fields in descriptive metadata records are included, excluding fields from structural, technical, rights, etc., metadata records. Sometimes, including a full-text index for this same search may be desirable, as described later in this chapter. It may not be desirable to include all the fields from a descriptive metadata record in a simple search index, however. Excluding fields from the simple search index should be the exception rather than the rule, but there are reasonable cases when this exception makes sense. Consider a system that contains published items. When a user types a place name into a simple search box, the vast majority of the time that user will be interested in a resource *about* that place rather than one published in that place. From this typical user's perspective, retrieving items that were published in that place but that have no other connection to the place results in irrelevant search results, and potentially a great many of them. Here, it would be a very reasonable decision to exclude publication place metadata from the simple search index, and provide publication place as a fielded search option (discussed in the next section) to meet the needs of those for whom this information is vital to discovery.

When determining which descriptive metadata fields to include in a simple search index, think about them one by one, considering what sort of query this metadata element would answer, which other fields in the metadata format used contain similar types of data, and how much redundancy exists between records in the system.[3] If inclusion of a field is likely to interfere with discovery of data in a different field and is unlikely to be a discovery target on its own, as in the publication place example above, exclude it from the search index. If the field contains data that is unlikely to be searched by end-users but is unlikely to interfere with searching for other data elements, consider including it in the simple search box regardless. A field such as a local ID number is unlikely to be known to end-users, but could be invaluable for project staff to quickly locate known items, and is unlikely to result in false hits for unrelated searches. Exclude fields from a simple search box carefully, but do not hesitate to do so when it is likely to improve the quality of search results.

Specialised search indexes

In addition to, and in some cases perhaps instead of, general keyword indexes, specialised search indexes may be appropriate for a digital library system. These specialised search indexes allow a user to perform a more precise and directed search, indicating, for example, that he wants a certain term to appear in a certain field in returned records. Choosing which specialised search indexes to implement isn't as simple as just picking fields from a metadata format, however. It will often be appropriate to group related fields from the native metadata format together into a single index, or to give the index a label for end-users that is different than the name of the field in the native metadata format.

Once again, understanding the discovery tasks with which users approach the system is a key element in making good decisions when designing search capabilities. Two major decisions must be made: which categories should be present as search options, and what granularity the indexes will represent. When deciding which categories to present as search options, an appropriate balance must be found between including all the options users are likely to need and keeping the list of options from becoming so long that it is difficult to use. In general, include data elements that are created to support discovery, and exclude data elements that solely provide contextual information designed to alert a user as to whether or not a resource is one they would like to learn more about. Include only indexes for fields that have data for a significant percentage of records in the system. It does not make sense for instance to offer users a search limit on visual resources if only half of the collection has an identified resource type.[4] The heterogeneity of metadata in a system will similarly affect which search indexes should be supplied. Shreeves et al. have identified significant differences in the use of simple Dublin Core fields across a wide range of cultural heritage institutions.[5] For example, in the museum community, many resources do not generally have titles, while in library collections they usually do. Other significant differences appear as well, including a notably longer average length of metadata records in the archival community than in museums or libraries.

Search indexes supporting both known-item discovery and unknown-item discovery are likely to be needed, although the types of material in a system may preference one over another. For example, a system consisting entirely of published works is much more likely to be the target of known-item queries than a system containing only unique documentary images. Indexes such as creator, title, and identifier tend to support known-item queries, whereas indexes such as subject, date, and resource type tend to support unknown-item, exploratory queries.

The appropriate granularity for search indexes is dependent on the type and scope of resources in the system. For some systems, a generic grouping of 'names' for all names of contributors, including both personal and corporate names, will be sufficient to meet user needs. For others, for example music, it may be necessary to provide specific name indexes for contributors with different roles, such as composer, arranger, and performer. For still other systems, both general and specific indexes will be needed and the search interface will need to make the relationship between them clear to the user. The OCLC FirstSearch interface to the WorldCat database (Figure 7.1) does this by utilising visual hierarchy within a combo box. Adding many specific categories to a list of search indexes can greatly increase the size of the list, so choose any more specific categories carefully to ensure their presence meets a user need that outweighs the detrimental effect of lengthening the list of choices.

Specialised search indexes can also be used in cases where a system contains full marked-up content of texts, finding aids, and so on. Features that are important in the markup of a specific type of resource, such as the recipient of a letter, the byline on a newspaper article, or the bulk dates of an archival collection, are good candidates for search indexes for systems containing these respective types of resources. In some cases, both a bibliographic and a full-text fielded search may be appropriate, and in others these functions could be combined into a single search interface. In either case, care must be taken to make it clear in the search interface the scope of what is being searched in the system once the user executes a query.

Figure 7.1 FirstSearch interface showing hierarchy between general and specific search indexes

Source: this screenshot is used with OCLC's permission. FirstSearch® is a registered trademark of OCLC. WorldCat® is a registered trademark and/or service mark of OCLC Online Computer Library Center, Inc.

Full-text indexing

Whether or not full text has received semantic markup, it can be indexed so that a user can perform a search against the full text of a resource rather than just bibliographic information about it. However, to make full-text indexing useful, sending a query to a simple word-for-word index of documents is likely to be insufficient. A digital library system implementing full-text indexing will likely want to use some of the many methods that have been developed to improve the performance of full-text retrieval systems.

Perhaps the most common method used to improve retrieval in full-text systems is the use of stop words, common terms such as 'and' that would likely match an extremely high percentage of documents in the collection. These terms are generally removed both from the full-text index and from queries submitted to the system. Another common technique for full-text indexing is stemming, a method which breaks down a word in a document or in a query to its root in order to match variants on the word, such as eat, eating, and eater. Many different stemming algorithms exist; some take a 'brute force' approach to removing characters, and others, such as lemmatisation, rely on lexical databases to take into account other factors such as the context and part of speech of a word to better determine its stem. Lexical databases such as WordNet[6] that encode relationships between words can also be used to expand queries to include results for documents that use synonyms for a query term and similar functionality. Other creative methods could be used to automatically expand the terms included in the index for a given document, such as examining other documents known to be related, using multi-lingual dictionaries to allow search terms in languages other than the document language, and so on. Ultimately, an index of 'full text' doesn't have to be (and possibly shouldn't be) exclusively an index of meticulously copied words from documents, but rather can be expanded far beyond into 'smarter' methods.

Another common feature of systems with full-text indexing is relevancy ranking of results. Information retrieval research[7] has long studied innovative means of improving retrieval and ranking of full-text documents, as can be seen through the work of the Text REtrieval Conference (TREC).[8] The growth of the Web has provided linkages between different documents, which can potentially be harvested to provide additional information on one document's relationship to another. Google's PageRank is the most notable current example of this phenomenon, relying heavily on links between Web documents to determine relevance.[9]

The methods used for querying and ranking results from full-text indexes don't necessarily have to be applied *only* to full-text indexes. Many metadata structure standards include a mixture of structured and unstructured fields. The unstructured elements contain free text, and potentially a great deal of it. If the information in those free-text metadata fields is deemed important for end-user discovery, a system could apply techniques from the full-text domain to the querying of text in certain structured metadata elements. The INitiative for the Evaluation of XML retrieval (INEX)[10] tests different approaches to adapt information retrieval algorithms to structured documents.[11] The most common approach used is to give metadata fields weights, with a relative importance assigned to each field. A match in a Title field might be considered more relevant than a match in a Relation field. In some cases, it is necessary to mix searches on metadata and the full text of documents.[12] In this case, the full text of the resource is assigned a relative importance, just as if it were any other metadata element.

Browsing

Browsing traditional hierarchies

Browsing offers a useful alternative to searching, in that it allows users to navigate through a collection according to a variety of predetermined categories. Browsing is convenient for users who come to a collection without a good idea of its contents, and for those who wish to see large sections of the collection at a glance. Browse categories may be similar to those chosen for search indexes, such as topic, author, or date, but others not used in a collection's search feature may be useful as well. The most useful browse categories are those that have a relatively small number of members, with each of the members having a large number of items within them.

Browsing categories, especially those based on controlled vocabularies or classification systems, are often hierarchical in nature. With a known hierarchy of information, a browse list could be presented to the user either in hierarchical mode, showing only the highest-level categories first and allowing the user to 'drill down' deeper into categories of interest, or in an alphabetical mode, showing all categories at any level of depth on a single alphabetical list. As the latter approach is often easier to implement, many collections use it, including the Library of Congress' American Memory collections,[13] most of which display a long alphabetic list of LCSH terms as a subject browse without showing any hierarchical relationships between them. The hierarchical mode of browsing provides some advantages for users over the alphabetical model in that it displays a much shorter list of initial options for categories to select, and provides more control for the user in selecting the desired depth of results. Some types of categories, such as geographical places, may lend themselves more naturally to presentation in a hierarchical manner than other categories. In either case, it is essential for the browsing models to show users results immediately, from the first browsing click. Further clicks can refine a result set, but the goal of browsing is to provide immediate access to the collection with a minimum of user action.

From a user interface point of view, browsing features typically appear as clickable links, rather than boxes requiring typing or combo boxes requiring selection of a value. The link model facilitates the overall goal of browsing to provide an at-a-glance view of the scope of a collection, whereas the other methods are not as effective at meeting this goal. Using existing classifications or controlled vocabularies for hierarchical browsing can result in unmanageably deep hierarchies, however. The well-known 'three clicks' rule in user interface design states that users should be able to find what they need in no more than three clicks. Although the validity of this rule is debatable,[14] and its applicability to this situation is unproven, it is important to keep in mind that users can get frustrated by hierarchical categories that are excessively deep.

Strict hierarchical models as browse categories also force a specific world-view on a collection. As argued by Clay Shirky,[15] information itself is not strictly hierarchical. Most resources will likely have more than one place in a hierarchical categorisation system, and browse features in digital library sites will likely need to accommodate this reality. As Shirky shows, for some types of resources the polyhierarchy can become so immense that it is no longer reasonably called a hierarchy, but rather a simple collection of links. Browsing categories can only provide one perspective on the intellectual content of a collection, but can still be useful for users as exploratory access points.

Facets: offering multiple entry points to the collection

Single browse categories are limited in that they only provide access to one feature of a collection at a time, such as the topic of a resource or a location it references. Faceted browsing, providing multiple categories that can be interactively combined, allow users to create their own desired view of a collection. The concept of faceting is not new; in fact, it traces at least as far back as Raganathan.[16] Marti Hearst describes faceted browsing in this way: 'The main idea is quite simple. Rather than creating one large category hierarchy, build a set of category hierarchies each of which corresponds to a different facet (dimension or feature type) relevant to the collection to be navigated'.[17] This approach is commonly used on commercial websites, but has only more recently gained favour in the cultural heritage sector. There is increasing evidence that users find the flexibility of discovery provided by faceted browsing to be a helpful means of discovery.[18]

While the use of faceted browsing in the cultural heritage sector is relatively recent, it has taken off quickly. The Gateway to 21st Century Skills group's Gateway to Educational Materials (GEM) initiative has developed multiple hierarchies of categories adapted to educational material by level of education, by instructional mediator, by type of resource, etc., as illustrated in Figure 7.2.[19]

Figure 7.2 Gateway to 21st Century Skills multiple browsing criteria

Browse by subject (glossary)   hide ▲

arts (3880) | educational technology (2238) | foreign languages (811) | health (3358) | language arts (5769) | mathematics (3960) | philosophy (346) | physical education (1806) | religion (523) | science (10626) | social studies (11043) | vocational education (411) |

Browse by type (glossary)   hide ▲

Activity (7637) | Artifact (186) | Best practice (456) | Catalog record (32) | Collection (3807) | Community (299) | Course (91) | Curriculum (348) | Curriculum support (2167) | Data set (338) | Environment (369) | Event (141) | Form (14) | Image set (202) | Lesson plan (9612) | Literature (2227) | Primary source (1343) | Project (491) | Realia (9) | Reference (1562) | Research study (201) | Secondary source (629) | Serial (252) | Service (124) | Story (120) | Study guide (209) | Test (2) | Tool (705) | Unit of instruction (1639) |

Browse by level (glossary)   show ▼

Browse by keywords (glossary)   hide ▲

American history (389) | Ancient Rome (488) | Ancient civilizations (441) | Communications (449) | Conservation (341) | Culture (350) | Drawing (418) | Economy (551) | Environment (497) | Geography (636) | Government (611) | History (342) | Internet (536) | Italy (519) | Maps (939) | Military (570) | NASA (365) | NASAexplores (592) | Natural resources (410) | People (551) | Plants (359) | Politics (407) | Population (348) | Roman Empire (432) | Romans (470) | Science (529) | Sound (359) | Transportation (623) | Water (587) | Weather (571) | More

Browse by mediator (glossary)   show ▼

Browse by beneficiary (glossary)   show ▼

Browse by priceCode (glossary)   show ▼

The Flamenco interface to the UC Berkeley Architecture Slides is an example of a faceted browsing interface that grew out of a research project into user behaviour.[20] Figure 7.3 shows a browse on the site of architectural images in North America, from the twentieth century, and showing exterior views. On the left-hand side of the screen, various navigation criteria related to the field of architecture are present to refine or change the results set: by people, period, location, structure type, material, style, view type, concept, etc. These facets are configurable for each collection presented by Flamenco. The Flamenco interface has been heavily tested with users; it has demonstrated its relevance for image retrieval. 'We have conducted a series of usability studies that find that, for browsing tasks especially, [faceted browsing] interfaces are overwhelmingly preferred over the standard keyword-and-results listing interfaces used in Web search engines [...]. Study participants find the design easy to understand, flexible, and less likely to result in dead ends'.[21]

Figure 7.3	Flamenco interface for UC Berkeley Architecture Image Library

The Endeca-powered library catalogue from North Carolina State University provides browsing on Library of Congress Classification number, then further faceting by topic, genre, format, library, region, era, language, and author.[22] Early usability tests on this system have been encouraging,[23] and the application of faceted browsing to the entirety of a library catalogue has inspired others to follow in North Carolina State's footsteps in moving towards providing this type of service.[24]

Advanced discovery functionality

User expectations are a strong driver of innovation in discovery functionality. A process called dominant design[25] describes the process by which at various points in the development of technology a specific combination of functions becomes a model for users. The Google 'box and a button' search page is an example of this phenomenon. Users today expect virtually all systems to use a query structure like Google's, with advanced functionalities such as quotes for searching a literal string available within a single search box. Given a new interface, despite any directions on the search page itself, users will tend to use Google-style syntax in a search box. Implementing features that allow these expectations to be successful will go a long way towards providing effective search results.

Many other methods are available for improving the retrieval performance of a digital library system. A few are outlined below, but this is not an exhaustive list. Select methods to implement in your system on the basis of their appropriateness to the types of resources included, and on sound user research demonstrating their effectiveness.

Query processing

Terms entered into a simple search box should not necessarily be searched as-is, directly on stored metadata. Various forms of query processing will likely be needed to conform to user expectations. In some cases, simple transformations from user language to system language, such as converting the name of a language to its coded form, are all that are needed. Similarly, dates should not be treated as literal strings, with the system looking for a strict date, formatted in just the same way as text fields. To enable more powerful date searching, such as resources that were created within a certain date range, dates must be identified as such in textual user queries, and sent to the appropriate date (not text string) indexes in the system, effectively accommodating resources described with date ranges rather than single dates.

Identifying names from a user query that potentially contains other information as well is a more difficult problem. A robust search system will be able to retrieve records that have been catalogued with an authoritative form of a name in response to a variety of name forms in user queries including 'First Last', 'Last, First', the omission of a middle initial when one is present in the authoritative form, and simple misspellings.

Reliably guessing the true intentions of a user from a simple free text query is challenging, and some would even describe it as impossible. If a user queries a system with the keyword 'Darwin', it is difficult to know whether the user is interested in resources that belong to a collection on Charles Darwin, have Charles Darwin as an author, are related to the Darwin-based Mac OS X operating system, or describe the Australian city. Data on a user's past system usage could be used to guess that the probability of one meaning of 'Darwin' is more likely than another, but collecting and managing data of this sort is a complex undertaking. Disambiguation features, such as those offered by Wikipedia,[26] are a much more frequent solution to this problem. Digital library systems in the cultural heritage sector generally take a conservative approach, making as few assumptions as possible on users' real intentions.

Thesaurus integration

Digital library systems that use controlled vocabularies or thesauri for metadata creation have traditionally only offered those vocabularies to users as a separate service, where a user searches the thesaurus itself, discovers an authorised term, then manually types that term into a query to the main system. Often the thesaurus is viewed or interacted with in a separate, pop-up window. More recent work has endeavoured to remove this separate search from the user's workflow, and integrate thesaurus structures into the search and browse engine itself. When integrating a thesaurus structure into a discovery system, a decision must be made as to when to use the thesaurus structure to *automatically* expand a query, and when to *interactively* expand it based on a user's request. Jane Greenberg has shown that synonyms and narrower terms in a controlled vocabulary are good candidates for automatic expansion, and broader and related terms are good candidates for interactive expansion.[27]

The Charles W. Cushman Photograph Collection from the Indiana University Office of University Archives and Records Management and the Indiana University Digital Library Program[28] implemented an integrated thesaurus search using the principles of query expansion outlined by Greenberg. On the Cushman site, queries are parsed to identify topical terms that match authorised or lead-in terminology from the Library of Congress' Thesaurus for Graphic Materials I: Subject Terms.[29] For each term identified, any lead-in term is automatically mapped to the authorised version of the term, showing the user that this was completed but not requiring an extra click or new search to be performed, and any authorised term (whether entered or matched by way of a lead-in term) is expanded to include all of its narrower terms in the search results retrieved. The search results are then displayed, along with the means to expand or restrict the result set with broader or narrower terms from the thesaurus for each matched term, without losing context provided by additional search terms.[30] Related terms could be treated in a similar way, as search suggestions displayed to the user.

Linking to similar resources

Expanding beyond items retrieved in one search to other 'similar' items is a common feature in modern retrieval systems. Perhaps the most difficult part of implementing a feature like this is determining what 'similar' means in the first place. A general definition presented by Sihna et al. describes related items as either sharing a property, or similar by content or similar by visit.[31] Simple connections like sharing the same value in a specific metadata element, such as author or topic, can be made to find similar resources. A system including the full text of resources can provide more advanced similarity analysis based on document content.

Similarity measures can also be based on community information. This type of information is used in recommendation systems based on user feedback. Similar data such as usage or circulation statistics could be used to implement these techniques for systems in the cultural heritage sector, as found in the The Melvyl Recommender Project performed by the California Digital Library.[32] Personal information stored in a user profile is yet another option for connecting an individual with additional relevant resources.

Links to similar items don't have to be limited to items within a single system. Citations in a journal article are one example of a feature that

Figure 7.4   National Science Digital Library[33]

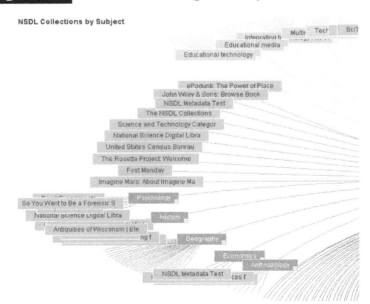

locates outside resources selected by humans as relevant to a source item. Methods that broadcast queries to outside systems are also possible. Formal protocols for linking and locating outside resources are described in Chapter 10.

Visual interfaces

The use of visual interfaces is on the rise as an alternative to textual searching and browsing. The National Science Digital Library, for example, offers a graphic interface to browse NSDL collections and categories, as illustrated in Figure 7.4.

Tag clouds (see Figure 7.5) offer a similar interface, displaying terms with a font size that is proportional to the number of resources having the term as attribute. Clouds are made either from full-text indexes or from metadata such as user tags. The terms are often presented in alphabetical order. The terms in tag clouds are not necessarily all of the same type, however. One study of tags used in del.icio.us categorised tags into seven types, including 'Identifying what (or who) it is about', 'Identifying qualities or characteristics' and 'Task organizing'.[34]

For particular types of information, more specific graphical interfaces can be developed. Historical timelines help locating dates and browsing historical periods as illustrated by the Metropolitan Museum of Art (see Figure 7.6).

Figure 7.5   LibraryThing tag cloud[35]

Figure 7.6 Historical timeline from the Metropolitan Museum[36]

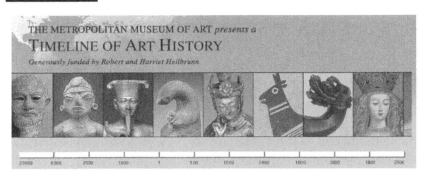

Spatial information can be effectively represented with maps (see Figure 7.7). Dynamic maps can be built using services such as the Google Map API or the Alexandria Digital Library Gazetteer Server.[37]

Results display

Sorting

Caroline and William Arms, in their chapter in the book *Metadata in Practice*, note that traditional measures of system performance such as

Figure 7.7 The world map representation corresponding to the part of the timeline that was selected from the Metropolitan Museum of Art[38]

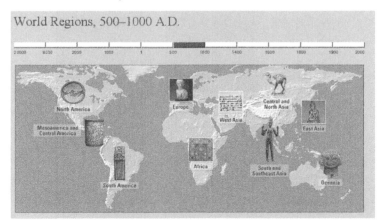

precision and recall are no longer the only means by which we should be evaluating our systems. Additional considerations such as ranking algorithms and user interface design must now receive our attention.[39] Indeed, experience with traditional search engines and the adaptation of user search behaviours to new system designs have showed that most users do not browse very deeply into a long results list. Giving users more control over the result set and returning the most relevant results at the top of the list is becoming more important than ever.

As discussed earlier in this chapter, relevance ranking can be an important feature of a digital library system. Relevance ranking becomes more difficult when too many metadata records in a system are overly similar,[40] or metadata records are too sparse to provide meaningful rankings. For many types of resources, alternatives to relevance ranking for sorting search results are useful. Consider offering results sorting for some subset of the search or browse indexes you have defined, especially by date and creator.

Snippets and contextual information

Snippets (short passages of text) are often included in results displays for textual works. The traditional Keyword in Context (KWIC) display shows a section of text in which a searched word is displayed, usually highlighted in some way, along with some text before and after the searched word. The goal of the snippet is to give the user enough information to select relevant resources of interest from the results set.

The principle of snippets can be used for non-textual works as well. A thumbnail-sized still image or key frame from a video could be used to supplement textual metadata to assist a user in determining if a search result is relevant to their need. For web pages, thumbshots (snapshots of the web page) have been shown to be helpful to users for recognising a website they have previously visited.[41]

Contextual information, such as which collection or subcollection the item belongs to, can be useful for users to assess the relevance of the item. The contextual information that should be provided depends on the nature of the resources themselves. There is anecdotal information to support, for example, the utility of including information about the colour of a book[42] to aid users in re-locating a resource they have used before. While many types of contextual information, such as the colour of a book, may be *useful*, each implementer must find the right balance between the vast set of information that *could* be provided, and what is *practical* to provide with available resources.

Another function of the snippet or other contextual information is to differentiate search results from one another. Enough information must be provided to allow a user to see the differences between items in the results set. Often, in a cross-collection search, many items from the same collection will be relevant to a single query. Users are frustrated if confronted with many pages of results from the same collection, as demonstrated by the experience of the University of Illinois at Urbana-Champaign.[43] A common approach to this issue is to only display a limited number of items from the same subcollection and offer users to see 'more results like this', similar to the search results display of Google when multiple pages from the same website are returned.

Managing results sets

In addition to presenting a simple list of items relevant to a query, a number of features can also be designed to allow better navigation within the results set, to disambiguate queries, or to easily modify the results set based on user actions. Clustering of results is the most common method in the first category, grouping related items together based on values in pre-determined metadata fields or with other methods from information retrieval research, such as document similarity or co-occurrence of terms from a user query. Figure 7.8 shows an example of

Figure 7.8 TouchGraph Google Browser that represents the connections between websites that contain the keyword Darwin[44]

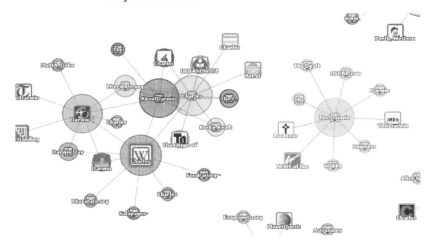

108

visual clusters built around the source website in which a query term appears. Clustering can also result in textual links to individual clusters rather than presentation in a visual interface. In either case, the goal is to provide the user with a high-level view of how the resources in the results set relate to one another, to aid in selecting the most relevant for further investigation.

As described earlier in this chapter, it is sometimes difficult to correctly interpret free text queries, especially if a system contains a large and diverse set of resources. In cases where a term has multiple meanings, query disambiguation techniques can be applied. Results could be displayed with each of the meanings in a separate cluster, or an intermediate step could be supplied asking the user to choose one of the possible meanings.

User-driven query refinement is another common technique used to help make better sense of a result set. This refinement could consist of broadening the scope of a query, narrowing it, or using what is seen in a result set to take the query in a slightly different direction. Query refinement can be performed in an interface in a number of different ways. One option, as described earlier in this chapter, is to use a controlled vocabulary to suggest broader, narrower, or related searches as links that a user might decide to click. Figure 7.9 shows a similar approach, mixing refining through additional facets with suggestions for related searches. Providing hyperlinks to new searches on the values in selected metadata fields in a search results display can allow a user to explore further an area that may not have been part of his original query. Common choices for hyperlinked data in results displays include creators, dates, subjects, and geographic places. Finally, a search box that allows a user to type new terms that will be added to the original query may be a useful way of providing user-driven query refinement.

Making sense of the many options

This chapter has summarised a large number of functionalities that could be offered by a digital library system. Trying to offer all of these functions, however, is neither practical nor likely to be user-friendly. Simple interfaces are often more efficient. Carefully choose the most relevant functions according to the objectives of the system, the target users, and the features of the resources themselves.

The available metadata can have a profound effect on the system functionality that can be provided. For example, most browsing

Figure 7.9 Exalead search engine[45] 'Narrow your search' on the keyword 'Darwin'

functions can only be supplied if enough metadata exists in a structured form, which is a challenge for local systems but an even greater one for distributed systems. It is best to plan system functionality while you are developing a metadata creation strategy, as each can inform the other.

Notes

1. Riley, J. and Dalmau, M. (2007) 'The IN Harmony Project: Developing a flexible metadata model for the description and discovery of sheet music', *The Electronic Library*, 25(2): 132–47.
2. Quam, E. (2001) 'Informing and evaluating a metadata initiative: usability and metadata studies in Minnesota's Foundations project', *Government Information Quarterly*, 18(3): 181–94.

3. Foulonneau, M. (2007) 'Information redundancy across metadata collections', *Information Processing and Management*, 43(3): 740–51. Available at *http://dx.doi.org/10.1016/j.ipm.2006.06.004*.
4. Foulonneau, M. and Cole, T.W. (2005) 'Strategies for reprocessing aggregated metadata', in *Proceedings Series: Lecture Notes in Computer Science*. Heidelberg: Springer-Verlag; pp. 290–301.
5. Shreeves, S.L., Kaczmarek, J.S. and Cole, T.W. (2003) 'Harvesting cultural heritage metadata using the OAI Protocol', *Library Hi Tech*, 21(2): 159–69.
6. Princeton University. 'WordNet – a lexical database for the English Language', available at *http://wordnet.princeton.edu/*.
7. Wikipedia entry on 'Information Retrieval'. Available at *http://en.wikipedia.org/wiki/Information_retrieval*.
8. National Institute of Standards and Technology, Text REtrieval Conference (TREC) (*http://trec.nist.gov/*).
9. Brin, S. and Page, L. (1998) 'The anatomy of a large-scale hypertextual web search engine', in Enslow, P.H. and Ellis, A. (eds) *Proceedings of the Seventh International Conference on World Wide Web* (Brisbane, Australia). Amsterdam, The Netherlands: Elsevier Science Publishers B.V.; pp. 107–17. Available at *http://www-db.stanford.edu/~backrub/google.html*.
10. Institut für Informatik und Interaktive Systeme, Universityof Duisburg. 'Initiative for the Evaluation of XML Retrieval', available at *http://inex.is.informatik.uni-duisburg.de/*.
11. Fuhr, N., Saadia, M. and Lalmas, M. (2003) 'Overview of the INitiative for the Evaluation of XML Retrieval (INEX) 2003', in *INEX 2003 Workshop Proceedings*, available at *http://inex.is.informatik.uni-duisburg.de:2003/proceedings.pdf*: pp. 1–11.
12. See for example: Sinha, V. and Karger, D.R. (2005) 'Magnet: supporting navigation in semistructured data environments', in *Proceedings of the 2005 ACM SIGMOD International Conference on Management of Data (Baltimore, Maryland, 14–16 Jun, 2005)*. SIGMOD; pp. 97–106. Available at *http://doi.acm.org/10.1145/1066157.1066169* or *http://haystack.lcs.mit.edu/papers/magnet-sigmod2005.pdf*.
13. Library of Congress. 'American memory', available at *http://memory.loc.gov/ammem/index.html*.
14. Porter, J. (2003) 'Testing the three-click rule', *User Interface Engineering*, available at *http://www.uie.com/articles/three_click_rule/*.
15. Shirky, C. (2005) 'Ontology is overrated', *Clay Shirky's Writings About the Internet*, available at *http://www.shirky.com/writings/ontology_overrated.html*.
16. Broughton, V. (2002) 'Facet analytical theory as a basis for a knowledge organization tool in a subject portal', in López-Huertas, M.J. and Muñoz-Fernández, F.J. (eds) *Challenges in Knowledge Representation and Organization for the 21st Century: Integration of Knowledge Across Boundaries: Proceedings of the Seventh International ISKO Conference, 10–13 July 2002, Granada, Spain*. Würzburg: Ergon Verlag; pp. 135–42. Available at *http://www.ucl.ac.uk/fatks/paper2.htm*.
17. Hearst, M.A (2006) 'Clustering versus faceted categories for information exploration', *Communications of the ACM*, 49(4): 59–61. Available at *http://flamenco.berkeley.edu/papers/cacm06.pdf*.

18. See, for example: Yee, K.-P., Swearingen, K., Li, K. and Hearst, M. (2003) 'Faceted metadata for image search and browsing', in *Proceedings of the SIGCHI Conference on Human Factors in Computing Systems (Ft. Lauderdale, Florida, USA, 05–10 April 2003)*. New York, NY: ACM Press; pp. 401–8. Available at *http://doi.acm.org/10.1145/642611.642681*.

19. Gateway to 21st Century Skills (*http://www.thegateway.org/browse*).

20. University of Berkeley School of Information. 'Flamenco UC Berkeley architecture slides', available at *http://orange.sims.berkeley.edu/cgi-bin/ flamenco.cgi/spiro/Flamenco?q=location:737/period:26/view_type:4&group= view_type*.

21. Hearst, M.A. (2006) 'Clustering versus faceted categories for information exploration', *Communications of the ACM*, 49(4): 59–61. Available at *http://flamenco.berkeley.edu/papers/cacm06.pdf*.

22. North Carolina State University. 'NCSU Libraries catalog', available at *http://www.lib.ncsu.edu/catalog/browse.html*.

23. Antelman, K., Lynema, E. and Pace, A.K. (2006) 'Toward a 21st century library catalog', *Information Technology and Libraries*, 25(3): 128–39. Available at *http://eprints.rclis.org/archive/00007332/*.

24. Florida Center for Library Automation. 'Combined catalog of the State University Libraries of Florida', available at *http://catalog.fcla.edu/*.

25. Anderson, P. and Tushman, M.L. (1990) 'Technological discontinuities and dominant designs: a cyclical model of technological change', *Administrative Science Quarterly*, 35(4): 604–33.

26. Wikipedia entry on 'Darwin'. Available at *http://en.wikipedia.org/wiki/ Darwin*.

27. Greenberg, J. (2001) 'Optimal query expansion (QE) processing methods with semantically encoded structured thesauri terminology', *Journal of the American Society for Information Science and Technology*, 52(6): 487–98.

28. Indiana University Charles W. Cushman Photograph Collection (*http://www.dlib.indiana.edu/collections/cushman/*).

29. Library of Congress. 'Thesaurus for graphic materials I: subject terms (TGM I)', available at *http://www.loc.gov/rr/print/tgm1/*.

30. Dalmau, M., Floyd, R., Jiao, D. and Riley, J. (2005) 'Integrating thesaurus relationships into search and browse in an online photograph collection', *Library Hi Tech*, 23(3): 425–52.

31. Sinha, V. and Karger, D.R. (2005) 'Magnet: supporting navigation in semistructured data environments', in *Proceedings of the 2005 ACM SIGMOD International Conference on Management of Data (Baltimore, Maryland, 14–16 Jun, 2005)*. SIGMOD; pp. 97–106. Available at *http://doi.acm.org/10.1145/1066157.1066169* or *http://haystack.lcs.mit .edu/papers/magnet-sigmod2005.pdf*.

32. Whitney, C. and Schiff, L. (2006) 'The Melvyl Recommender Project: developing library recommendation services', *D-Lib Magazine*, 12(12): available at *http://www.dlib.org/dlib/december06/whitney/12whitney.html*.

33. National Science Digital Libraries. 'NSDL collections by subject', available at *http://nsdl.org/browse/ataglance/browseBySubject.html*.

34. Golder, S.A. and Huberman, B.A. (2006) 'The structure of collaborative tagging systems', *Journal of Information Science*, 32(2): 198–208.

35. LibraryThing (*http://www.librarything.com/tagcloud.php*).
36. Metropolitan Museum of Art. 'Timeline of art history', available at *http://www.metmuseum.org/toah/*.
37. University of California Santa Barbara. 'Alexandria Digital Library Gazetteer server client. Using ADL server', available at *http://middleware .alexandria.ucsb.edu/client/gaz/adl/index.jsp*.
38. The Metropolitan Museum of Art. 'Timeline of art history – world regions, 500–1000 A.D.', available at *http://www.metmuseum.org/toah/hm/06/ hm06.htm*.
39. Arms, C. and Arms, W.Y. (2004) 'Mixed content and mixed metadata: information discovery in a messy world', in *Metadata in Practice*. Chicago, IL: American Library Association.
40. Foulonneau, M. (2007) 'Information redundancy across metadata collections', *Information Processing and Management*, 43(3): 740–51. Available at *http://dx.doi.org/10.1016/j.ipm.2006.06.004*.
41. Dziadosz, S. and Chandrasekar, R. (2002) 'Do thumbnail previews help users make better relevance decisions about web search results?', in *Proceedings of the 25th Annual International ACM SIGIR Conference on Research and Development in Information Retrieval*. Tampere, Finland: ACM; pp. 365–6. Available at *http://doi.acm.org/10.1145/564376.564446*.
42. Shirky, C. (2005) 'Ontology is overrated', *Clay Shirky's Writings About the Internet*, available at *http://www.shirky.com/writings/ontology_overrated .html*.
43. Shreeves, S.L. and Kirkham, C.M. (2004) 'Experiences of educators using a portal of aggregated metadata', *Journal of Digital Information*, 5(3): available at *http://jodi.tamu.edu/Articles/v05/i03/Shreeves/*.
44. Touchgraph. 'Touchgraph Google Browser', available at *http://www .touchgraph.com/TGGoogleBrowser.html* (search for 'darwin' shown in text).
45. Exalead (*http://www.exalead.com*).

Part IV
Metadata interoperability

Resource sharing is often not a top priority for cultural heritage institutions. Nevertheless, digital projects are increasingly making resources held by these institutions openly available on the Internet. As soon as these resources go live, they are accessible through services maintained by third parties: other institutions, individuals, or commercial companies. Such third party services include Web portals, search engines, and the like. The institution that makes available the digital resources and their metadata has only limited means for controlling the way third parties use or represent these resources.

Metadata plays a large part in facilitating the sharing of digital objects. As seen in Parts II and III of this book, the implementation of a metadata strategy affects the use to which those records can be effectively put. In this environment, metadata records can be refocused and reprocessed to be 'shareable', that is, more easily usable by third party systems.

Part IV of this book discusses the role of metadata design in establishing interoperability between a collection of digital resources and a service. Chapter 8 describes the main principles of interoperability. Chapter 9 considers the ways in which third party systems can use metadata to facilitate resource discovery. Chapter 10 provides an overview of the primary standards and technologies that are used to share metadata and content with third party systems. Finally, Chapter 11 shows how it is possible to design and reprocess metadata to improve its usability by third party systems.

8

Defining interoperability

Why sharing?

Individual institutions have developed a multiplicity of online services to highlight the value of their content and allow users to interact with their collections. Those services are often implemented locally. For example, most libraries now offer a website that provides access to an online catalogue of their resources. However, in addition to local services, other services can be built collaboratively with other institutions. In this case, digital content from one institution can be made available through a number of different types of applications, many of which could not have been developed by the institution that holds the content alone. A third-party search engine is one example of this phenomenon, adding value to local content by improving its discoverability.

The Australian National Archives recognises the impact of having shared its metadata with other Australian institutions to build a single access point to photographic collections of Australia: 'From September 2000, website visits were boosted by the inclusion of our photographic database, PhotoSearch, in the PictureAustralia website maintained by the National Library. This website offers a single point of access to some of Australia's largest pictorial collections. In the first month of operation, almost 100,000 visitors accessed PhotoSearch on our website via PictureAustralia'.[1]

Those shared applications can provide new opportunities to increase the audience of individual collections. Individual institutions do not always have the expertise to develop multiple systems for different audiences. A shared service might be designed for a different audience than the one originally envisioned by the holding institution, which would allow new users to discover a collection. Collaborative services can provide new access points or new tools to manipulate content. They can also propose new ways of grouping resources, based on relationships between collections. By gathering different collections and representing them in a new context, they can suggest a new interpretation of the content. In addition, collaborative services help better focus an individual institution's efforts and investment. An institution can invest once in sharing a collection, and then benefit from multiple services built by others on top of that collection.

Collections and services

At the heart of collaboration lies the harmonisation of collections and services. In this context, a *service* is an application that allows the performance of any task or function as explained in Chapter 6. A *collection* is a set of digital or physical resources that is curated using defined guiding rules or principles. A website, then, is a service that publishes a collection of resources.

Many cultural and academic institutions are willing to share information about their physical or digital collections. With this shared information, collaborative services can be developed to enhance retrieval, access, and manipulation of digital collections. For example, a clustering service developed by Emory University demonstrates a methodology that could be used to build browse interfaces on disparate metadata.[2] The service clusters the resources based on existing metadata records; the institution that holds the collections only has to share its metadata. No technical competence at the sharing institution is required to develop and manage a clustering tool in order to provide this service. Value can also be added by the bringing together of distributed resources all related to the same topic, as seen in the California Digital Library's American West project.[3] In this project, metadata from a number of collections from institutions spanning the United States was harvested, and an effort was made to select from the entirety of the harvested metadata only those resources that related to the American West. Such a service could present these disparate resources together, highlighting each in the context of the history of a specific geographic area. Unfortunately, the American West project did not result in a publicly-available, searchable aggregation of the targeted resources, but it does nonetheless demonstrate how services can cast a new light on a collection or a resource not envisioned by the original holding institution.

Not all institutions have the capability or the will to maintain or even create both content and applications. Certain institutions, because of their primary curatorial responsibility, will likely concentrate their efforts on the content, its selection, its traceability, its authenticity and its integrity. Institutions that are involved in the provision of digital services must make sure that advanced applications highlight the value of that content. They must create new value by enhancing the original context of resources.

Open architectures allow this sort of distribution of responsibilities between content and service providers, making it possible to connect content hosted in multiple locations with services hosted in yet other locations. As an example, a meta-search service called the 'Grainger Engineering Library Search Aid for Engineering and Business Information'[4] is hosted on a server at the University of Illinois at Urbana-Champaign. It however provides access to collections that are hosted all over the world on multiple servers. It even queries other distant services such as Google or the ISI Web of Science. This distribution of collections and services, where the content and the application may be hosted in distinct locations, allows the responsibility for the final products and services delivered to users to be shared across multiple institutions.

Facets of interoperability

Interoperability, at its most basic level, is the ability of different systems to talk to each other.[5] The collaboration between multiple institutions and the creation and maintenance of collections and applications by different players requires the definition of mechanisms to connect content and applications across networks. In order to enable interactions between different systems, it is necessary to define a common language. These systems must be able to exchange and interpret information. For example, if System A hosts a collection of digital resources and System B hosts a search/retrieval service, System A needs to send to System B all necessary information for System B to include the collection in the service. System B must be able not only to receive and store the message sent by System A, but also to process and interpret it. This is usually accomplished by adding interoperability layers on both systems to translate their internal information into a common language.

Technical interoperability: reading the message

If System A sends information across a network to System B, the first challenge is to make sure that System B will receive and decode the data. Protocols are the technical mechanisms that define rules for transporting data and making sure that the data can be encoded at one end and decoded at the other end of the transfer. For example, the TCP/IP protocols define principles used on the World Wide Web.

Data can be encoded in a format such as XML to be sent over the network. This can allow the sender to structure the information contained in the package. However, if the receiver does not have an application which reads and interprets the codes used by the XML language (an XML parser), then System B cannot read the message sent by System A. In a similar vein, a PDF document is likely to be readable by multiple target systems because the codes or language used to represent information in the PDF format are interpretable by a number of different 'reader' software packages, including those available from Adobe.

Content-related interoperability: interpreting the message

Metadata, as structured data about resources, enables user and system interactions with the resources themselves. Even if the data transmitted is correctly read by System B, it must still be interpreted. For example, consider a case where System A is willing to share the information that a document was created on '04/01/06'. System B, in order to interpret this message correctly, must have additional information at its disposal.

Semantic interoperability

The system must first identify that this information represents a date, more specifically the creation date of the document. The nature of the information must be specified somewhere along the transfer chain. Typically, an XML encoding can define the semantics of information contained in the document. For example, the Date element of the Dublin Core Metadata Element Set can represent this information as <dc:date>04/01/06</dc:date>. The Dublin Core data dictionary defines the Date element as 'A date of an event in the lifecycle of the resource'.[6] Referencing this definition does not remove all ambiguities as it does not specify which date is represented (creation, publication, etc.) but this human-readable definition provides a first level of semantic interpretability.

Syntactic interoperability

Even if System B receives '04/01/06' and knows this is a date, it still has to interpret that date. If the system does not have any other information at its disposal, it will encounter difficulties in determining with certainty whether this is January 4th 2006, April 1st 2006, or one of those days in the year 1906. However, if the system knows that the first part represents the month, the second part the day and the third part the year of the current century, then it is possible to state with certainty that this date is actually the 1st of April 2006.

In order to facilitate syntactic interoperability, it must be possible to state which encoding scheme was used to encode the information. The date 2004-05-02 can be interpreted correctly if the system knows that this date was encoded according to the set of rules defined by the W3C Date and Time Format (W3C-DTF):[7] YYYY-MM-DD.

Linguistic interoperability

Even if System B knows that a date will be encoded as DD-Month-YYYY (day, month spelled out, and year), both 01-January-2006 and 01-Enero-2006 would be compliant. However, these two options use different languages to indicate the month. System B therefore needs to be able to identify that 'Enero' is a Spanish term. Then it needs to translate that term into the system language. Differences between languages occur most often for subjects, place names, and so on. Many digital documents and metadata records are even encoded using multiple languages. The identification of the language used to write every piece of information in a document can therefore be a challenge. Even within a single language, words can be open to multiple interpretations. The date boundaries of the Middle Ages, for example, are drawn at different times for different countries and for different knowledge domains.

The entity the data relates to

Outside of its relevant context, it is impossible for System B to do anything with data it receives unless it knows what it is about. The most common case is not that a system receives a date out of any context but that a system expects a date about an object, yet receives, for example, a date which relates to a group of objects or a part of an object. It is a challenge for System B to do anything useful with that date – for example, extrapolate that the date also applies to the object itself. Another very common case is the ambiguity between physical and digital resource descriptions. Many metadata records mix information about the digital and the physical object when relating to analogue objects that have been digitised. Is the date supplied the date of creation of the picture or the date of creation of the object (e.g., a monument) depicted in the picture? A shared understanding of the object of description must exist between System A and System B. Unique and persistent object identifiers are one common means of addressing this ambiguity.

Organisational interoperability: synchronising message transfers

Organisation of people, responsibilities and knowledge is a key component of interoperability, because it defines who and what will intervene to make communication between systems possible. The dialogue between two systems cannot work appropriately if the flow of information is not handled in a similar manner in both systems. If data is to be synchronised between two systems hosted in different institutions, the internal organisation of those institutions has a major role in ensuring the smooth completion of the process. Difficulties can arise due to differing organisational structures: for example when one person is responsible for the maintenance of the system in one institution, while a number of persons are responsible of different aspects of the system in another institution. In other cases, the person in charge only has the mission of rebooting a server and identifying issues but cannot modify the application in cases where an error is identified. The person can also have exclusively technical competences in one institution, whereas the person in charge at another institution has exclusively content-related competences. Any modification in system processes will require both institutions to assemble all the relevant individuals with the competencies necessary to make the modification. The speed at which the institutions can react to changes may also be wildly different.

Another example of challenges to organisational interoperability can be seen in the case of learning management systems. These systems usually gather material for specific educational curricula and identify audiences for those collections in terms of level or age. However, different countries have different educational systems. Similar resources can be part of curricula in the UK for a specific grade level but of different curricula and even different grade levels in Oregon. Similar issues arise with regard to institutional repositories. In France, many research laboratories exist, each affiliated with different institutions including universities, research institutes and ministries. As a result, the concept of institutional repositories is harder to match to institutional repositories from other countries where researchers are more often affiliated with a single institution.

The challenge of making collections usable by multiple systems

Metadata standards can help systems communicate. Technical metadata, for example, supports usage transactions between systems. Descriptive metadata for digital objects allows discovery services. Layers added to systems usually allow the translation of information from its local representation into one that can be interpreted in the other system. Those layers ensure the presence of additional information, which allows the interpretation of the transferred message. For example, '06' in a database exclusively containing twentieth century literature is not an ambiguous year. However, when transferred to another system, it needs to be re-encoded to be more explicit, i.e. as '1906'. The date 1906-02-02 must be supplemented by the indication that the information follows the syntax specified by the W3CDTF standard. This information on the rules that should be applied to transferred data is necessary for a second system to interpret it.

Sometimes, a system receiving data does not have the capability to look for interpretation rules and apply them in order to decode and interpret the data transferred. In many cases, even if System A sends a date with the indication that it is compliant with the rules defined in the ISO 8601 'Representation of dates and times'[8] standard, it may not be interpreted properly by System B. As ISO 8601 includes a wide variety of cases and possible encodings, System B will very possibly not have at its disposal a program that can interpret all the rules of the ISO 8601. While System B may be able to resolve most cases of ISO 8601 encoding, it may not be able to interpret a particular date with certainty.

Interoperability is not only about documenting all the information sent through a transaction. Effective communication is only possible if the other system also has the capabilities to interpret this information. There is no perfectly interoperable system, able to talk to all possible others without loss of data. Any given system can only truly interoperate with a subset of other possible systems.

This leads to a major challenge for improving systems interoperability. The necessary communication between systems is growing at an astonishing rate, and the number of online collections and services available is also increasing. It becomes very difficult for a system to simultaneously take into account the capabilities of all the systems willing to interact with it. Indeed, either a system must share its data in a different way for each individual system it wants to interact with, or it has to share content in one way (or a small number of ways), designed to meet the needs of the systems having the lowest technical capabilities. This second strategy, however, can greatly limit the usability of the data in the other system. This phenomenon is frequently seen with implementers of the Open Archives Protocol for Metadata Harvesting (OAI-PMH). The OAI-PMH protocol requires all resources have metadata available in Simple Dublin Core, and encourages communities to supplement this simple metadata format with additional formats useful for that community or that type of resource. The OAI-PMH designers implemented this requirement in the hope that mandating one metadata format would provide a baseline of interoperability across systems. Because of the requirement of OAI-PMH for Simple Dublin Core, many content providers originally shared their data *only* in that format, and many OAI-PMH-compliant software packages could only deal with Simple Dublin Core and nothing else. However, using only this format can leave many ambiguities in shared data. For example, it is not possible to state unequivocally which date is represented (creation, publication, etc) in a Simple Dublin Core record. The usability of this data in another system can therefore be limited.

A system may support different levels of interoperability with different systems. Collection providers should design a 'sharing strategy' for their content. This should include a 'metadata sharing strategy' that takes into account various levels of expectations from the systems it can have to share data with now or in the future. It is generally good practice to share, in addition to any other desired formats, the most complete descriptive metadata records available. However, not all systems will have the capability of interpreting these more complete records. A good solution is to offer a simple format such as Dublin Core, and supplement this with a more robust one appropriate to your environment, such as MARC or MODS in a library. Additional formats for specific systems or types of resources can also be designed.

Interoperable records conform to the expectations of the target system. If a system shares LC or Dewey classification information, it can use a code such as BQ indicating an LC classification. Coded data is more precise than textual data, and is a good way of unambiguously representing a piece of data. However, if the receiving system does not have the necessary capability to decode that information, then it will not be able to use it. Therefore, for certain types of target systems, 'Buddhism' can be a more appropriate way of sharing this same information. In cases where the target system is able to interpret the textual data, it may be able to relate it to the appropriate code; otherwise, it can still use it as general information on the area of knowledge the resource is about.

Balancing interoperability with local needs

Very often, content providers who share collections on the Web must adapt their local metadata in order to share it and make it available to other systems. Indeed, systems are often not primarily designed to interact with each other. They are more likely designed to carry out a local mission, such as creating a local catalogue or supporting a website. When collections are shared, they are generally re-purposed. Metadata created for a specific usage model must be transformed and re-adapted to enable interactions with resources in a different context. Transformation carries with it a risk of misuse of information, but this process lies at the core of content-related interoperability. Metadata plays a major role in enabling systems interoperability and, therefore, the creation of new services on the Web. It is necessary to define a metadata sharing strategy, as described in Chapter 11, to adapt metadata for many different contexts and to re-purpose it for use in a multiplicity of systems.

Notes

1. National Archives of Australia (2001) *Annual report 2001*. Available at *http://www.naa.gov.au/publications/corporate_publications/ar2001/outcomes_outputs_reports2.html*.
2. See *http://metacombine.org/web_services/cluster-server.wsdl* and Krowne, A. and Halbert, M. (2005) 'An initial evaluation of automated organization for digital library browsing', in *Proceedings of the 5th ACM/IEEE-CS Joint Conference on Digital Libraries (Denver, CO, USA, 07–11 Jun, 2005)*. New York, NY: ACM Press; pp. 246–255. Available at *http://doi.acm.org/10.1145/1065385.1065442*.
3. California Digital Library. 'New frontiers in the digital library: social and ecological diversity of the American West', available at *http://www.cdlib.org/inside/projects/amwest/*.
4. University of Illinois at Urbana-Champaign Grainger Engineering Library search aid for engineering and business information (*http://susanowo.grainger.uiuc.edu/searchaid/searchaid.asp*).

5. See Foulonneau, M. (2005) 'L'interopérabilité des systèmes documentaires', in Aubry, C. and Janik, J. (eds) *Les Archives Ouvertes: Enjeux et Pratiques. Guide à l'Usage des Professionnels de l'Information*. Paris: ADBS.

6. Dublin Core Metadata Initiative. 'Dublin Core metadata element set, Version 1.1', available at *http://dublincore.org/documents/dces/*.

7. Wolf, M. and Wicksteed, C. (1997) 'Date and Time formats', *W3C*, available at *http://www.w3.org/TR/NOTE-datetime*.

8. International Organization for Standardization. 'Numeric representations of dates and times – the ISO solution to a long-standing source of confusion', available at *http://www.iso.org/iso/en/prods-services/popstds/datesandtime.html*.

9

Interoperability and resource discovery

An institution will likely consider internal requirements as the primary driver of metadata decisions. The first objective is generally to provide access to local users, manage local content or preserve local resources. However, more and more, institutions make their local system directly available on the Web to users anywhere. A major motivation for institutions in publishing their content on the Web is to improve the discoverability of their resources by existing users as well as by new users. Sometimes, a dispersed audience was originally targeted, but sometimes, additional audiences are found only after metadata and resources have been made available. In any case, metadata plays a major role in enlarging the original audience of the content through tools available on the Internet.

Resource discovery

Resource discovery focuses on guaranteeing that a user will have knowledge of the existence and relevance of a resource whenever appropriate. In a digital library system, discovery can be thought of as supported by a number of functions, such as *Find* a relevant resource, *Rank* that resource, *Present* that resource in a list of results or in a browsing interface in such a manner that it may be selected by a user as a resource of potential interest.

Making a resource discoverable is not only about making it available on the Web. If the content provider considers that a resource or collection of resources is worth discovering, the resource or collection should be addressable by portals, search engines, and services that provide access to distributed content. The local system's location and availability should be broadcast to those services likely to make best use of the content in that system. Many techniques could be used together to most effectively broadcast this information, including search engine optimisation techniques, communication with the main portals and services in the primary domain interested in the resources, facilitating auto-discovery mechanisms that allow a browser to identify a repository and so on. In each of these cases, appropriate technologies, such as those for sharing metadata, should be implemented to optimise access to the resources by the remote service.

When metadata is used by remote systems, it is sometimes difficult to know how a system will use that metadata to provide discovery services (see Chapter 6 for one example of how to learn about this, involving 'radioactive records'). Whenever possible, the specific functions implemented in a remote system should be investigated in order to operate appropriate transformations of the data for that system, or to take any other appropriate action.

Resource discovery in other connected systems

An improvement of the discoverability of an institution's resources is a common rationale given for taking the time to make local systems interoperable. The implementation of an OAI-PMH repository (as described in Chapter 10) to share metadata has been proven to increase significantly the visits on a website. For example, at the State Library of New South Wales, in 2002/2003 there were 2,960,665 requests for pages referred by PictureAustralia (a cross-domain portal that uses OAI-PMH), representing 37% of the total requests for pages to State Library image server. A similar phenomenon happened for the Australian National Archives as noted in Chapter 8. The technologies remote services use to access the information they need can vary considerably. They can use federated search mechanisms, harvesting, or spidering techniques to access the information available for each resource (see Chapter 10 for more information on specific protocols based on these models).

The inclusion of a digital collection in a network of repositories that share a common communication protocol allows users to discover a resource from distributed sites. Cross-repository services represent the content in a different context than the one used at a local institution.

For example, a user can discover a sound record of a toad call at the Animal Diversity Web website of the University of Michigan Museum of Zoology[1] or in the OAIster database of digital resources.[2] In each of these repositories, the context in which the resource is presented is slightly different. The user community considered by each system is potentially different as well.

If a record is present in as many systems as possible, then the resource has more chances to be discovered. If the data used by each of those systems is well adapted to the functions implemented by that system, then the resource has an even greater chance to be discovered. As seen in Figure 9.1, not all remote systems use the same information, nor do they provide the same functionality.

Certain services do not use metadata at all but only the full text of resources, and thus only operate on resources with a textual component. Others only index web pages, or only display website descriptions or collection-level descriptions. Some rely on external criteria such as popularity, while still others use two or more of those elements. The digital image resource presented in the centre of Figure 9.1 can be accessed through a local interface as well as a number of other applications which all use different information to provide access to that digital resource (OAIster, the IMLS digital collections registry,[3] the CIC metadata portal,[4] and Google). Metadata is only part of the material

Figure 9.1 Different applications use different information about digital resources

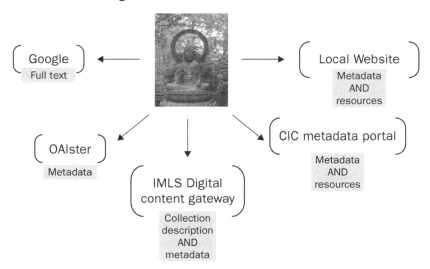

used by discovery services. As more and more systems are developed in the future, it is likely this variety of approaches will continue to expand, and different information will support many alternative ways to discover and access resources.

Remote services also implement different methods for discovering the existence of new information sources. These can involve action from a local institution such as making a declaration to registry designed for this purpose, sending messages to professional mailing lists, providing a direct declaration to the service provider, or participating in auto-discovery mechanisms that allow a spider or a browser to identify that there is an information source it can access.

Generalist search engines

Originally, search engines on the Web used metadata to discover and index Web resources. The HTML language includes invisible META tags such as TITLE, DESCRIPTION and KEYWORD. Those metatags provide to machines (typically search engines) information about a web page.

Web page authors originally provided such tags in order to allow search engines to correctly process their web pages. The Dublin Core metadata format was created in this context. The creation of minimal standards to record metatags had the potential to provide richer discovery functions. One of its potential applications was to structure the digital resources descriptions (like web pages) in META tags, following the structure <META NAME="DC.CREATOR" CONTENT="Smith, Dan">. This would be one way of including a limited level of bibliographic information structuring on the Web. The inclusion of Dublin Core metadata elements in HTML 2.0 META tags was notably discussed[5] as an issue for the future of Web indexing.

Major search engines used META tags according to slightly different rules, limiting for example the length of the content of the DESCRIPTION tag they would index. Web page authors were expected to provide a description of their own resources. As a result, a large proportion of the META tags on the Web were used more as advertising than as 'bibliographic' information. A bibliographic approach would leave all resources an equal chance (theoretically) to be discovered by as many interested users as possible. Instead of developing metadata in order to be able to obtain the best match between a resource and a query (information demand), the META tags became too often a competition to attract as many people as possible to the resource created, whether those people were interested or not in the resource.

Search engine optimisation techniques in this context led to the inclusion of keywords that have nothing to do with the resource. A typical abuse would be a religious website including sexually-oriented keywords in order to give a message to users looking for pornographic content on the Web. Richard A. Spinello summarises this as 'manipulative activities interfere with the efficient search and retrieval of information on the Web, as they tend to yield search results that are overinclusive'.[6] To limit the impact of this sort of abuse, search engines soon turned to methods that analyse page content rather than placing a great deal of trust in the content of META tags.

Today, it is generally accepted that most search engines still pay attention to the web page <title> tags, suggesting that web page authors should provide meaningful and differentiated page titles to their resources. When pages are published from a Web content management system, it can be useful to generate a title tag for the web page, either the same one for the whole collection or a distinct one for all resources in the collection. When the title is not meaningful out of context, it may still be possible to create meaning with the combination of the website title and the resource title.

Search engines, however, are not always able to discover all publicly-accessible resources. Search engines typically discover new resources to index by following links between web pages. This mechanism is well adapted to static websites for which a link was created in one page or another to all individual pages of the website. Software robots follow links to discover new pages and index them. However, many institutions such as museums, photo agencies, libraries, and archives put on the Web resources stored in repositories. In such repositories, resources are discovered thanks to internal indexes rather than links. Without an explicit link to a document, a robot cannot find a resource in order to index it. The set of resources which are available on the Web but that are generated dynamically and not indexed by search engines is called the 'Deep Web'. It was estimated in 2001 that the size of the Deep Web was 450 to 500 times the number of pages indexed by search engines.[7]

The key difficulty in indexing the Deep Web is learning the identifiers of individual resources. For example a resource can be addressed with a URL such as: *http://mydatabase.org/findmyresource.php?resource Identifier=637*. All pages on this server are available, if only the search engine knew the resource identifiers that would result in obtaining web pages. Search engines have now progressed in indexing dynamic pages on the Web, but they still often only index partially the content of databases.

Various techniques exist to make resources stored in a database available to general Web search engines. For example, Google suggests that webmasters create sitemaps to assist in sharing a complete picture of a site for indexing.[8] A sitemap is a list of URLs to all resources of the database in a standard form, stored in a file at a specific location with a specific name, so that a search engine can discover it, read it, and access all the URLs it contains for indexing purposes. The use of sitemaps goes beyond the Google search engine, however, as in November 2006 a common sitemap format in XML was announced that is supported by Yahoo!, Google, and MSN.[9,10] This sitemap protocol allows the specification of pages of a website and administrative metadata that supports efficient indexing by search engines and can contain up to 50,000 URLs. Each URL of the website can have optional properties: the last modification date, the frequency of update, and the priority. The priority metadata is only used to discriminate between URLs within the same site. For example, if multiple pages of the same site match the request and the website creator has assigned priorities to each web page, then this information can be used to rank the results. Box 9.1 shows the structure of a sitemap. A sitemap index can be created if necessary in order to allow a search engine to access multiple sitemaps.

Google also offers webmasters the option to store metadata records in an OAI-PMH data provider, again stored at a specific location (directly

Box 9.1   Example of an XML sitemap

```
<?xml version="1.0" encoding="UTF-8"?>
<urlset xmlns="http://www.sitemaps.org/schemas/
sitemap/0.9">
<url>
<loc>http://www.mypage.org</loc>
<lastmod>2007-03-08</lastmod>
<changefreq>daily</changefreq>
<priority>0.7</priority>
</url>
</urlset>
```

below the server root directory).[11] The search engine can harvest the content of the OAI-PMH data providers and use any URLs present as targets for indexing.

The search engines Yahoo! and Google have entered into agreements to collect the metadata records from the University of Michigan OAIster service, which attempts to harvest all OAI-PMH records for digital resources freely available on the Web.[12] It seems, however, that the OAI-PMH records are used by these search engines simply to discover URLs of resources they might otherwise miss, rather than as a source of structured descriptive metadata. In 2004, Frank McCown, Xiaoming Liu, Michael Nelson and Mohammad Zubair at Old Dominion University isolated samples of OAI-PMH records for online resources in order to learn more about the interaction of OAI-PMH with Web search engines. They used values from the Dublin Core identifier field in OAI-PMH records to query MSN, Google and Yahoo! to identify whether these search engines had indexed the resources available in OAI-PMH compliant repositories. The rate of resources actually indexed, taking into account the fact that new resources require a delay for being indexed and searchable on the engine, was fairly high but unequal across search engines. For example, from the Perseus digital library (texts in the humanities), Google indexed 9.2%, Yahoo! 99.6% and MSN did not index any of the URLs. From the CERN document server (ePrints), 74.5% were indexed by Google, 27.4% by Yahoo!, and 3.9% by MSN. Overall, the authors conclude that 'of the 3.3M unique web resources described in the Dublin Core metadata available through OAI-PMH repositories, approximately 700K (21%) were not indexed by any search engine. Yahoo! indexed the most (65%), followed by Google (44%) and MSN (7%)'. The authors highlight the role of the agreement with Yahoo! and the presence of robot.txt files in certain collections that prevent robots from indexing the resources of a given website.[13]

The methods search engines use for locating resources for indexing change over time and adapt to new behaviours of Web resources creators.[14] For example, as search engines began to use backlinks to measure the interest of a website (number of pages that include a link to the resource), link farms appeared which had no function other than to generate higher ranking measures for search engines. Search engines also have adopted measures to avoid indexing the same resource multiple times when it appears at different URLs, such as mirror sites. Certain search engines run similarity algorithms to identify 'near-duplicate' pages. Metadata records for individual resources within a collection are sometimes extremely similar, and search engines tend to define similarity of resources according to the similarity of their textual content.[15] Very similar metadata records could appear to a search engine as a single resource, when in fact they represent multiple resources.

Despite all of these complications, there are some general approaches that content providers can use to make their materials more search engine-friendly. While search engines give META tags much less weight than in the past, or even none at all, the TITLE metatag is still considered important information by most search engines. The usage of DESCRIPTION and KEYWORD tags depends on the search engine considered. A short description and several non-repetitive keywords in these tags can, however, support effective processing of the resource by search engines. The creation of a sitemap or an OAI-PMH data provider for resources is also recommended as methods to ensure a search engine can find all of an institution's relevant content.

Despite the focus on indexing the full text of Web content, metadata still has a role in facilitating the indexing of resources. Generally, the best approach is to pay careful attention to the URLs stored in metadata records, as these are one of the major entry points to the resources for search engines. It is therefore very important to make sure that the URL stored in a metadata record (particularly in the Identifier field for Dublin Core records) is pointing to a relevant view of the resource.

The design of the web pages, the generation of differentiating information on pages describing resources, and similar, are other factors for the discovery of such resources. For non-textual resources, a search engine may include metadata displayed with the resource as part of its search index. It is essential, therefore, to provide information about the resource, such as a distinct title, on each web page, as well as meta-information, for example, in an <img alt=" "> attribute.

Portals and registries

Web portals, directories and registries are some of the many ways of providing discovery services based not on searching mechanisms but rather on browsing capabilities, which allow users to explore a range of useful clusters of resources. Typically these services do not provide access to individual objects, but rather to either a group of objects available from a database or a full website. Portals usually allow users to search, browse and select resources based on a collection-level description of the content or a description of a complete website.

Although websites can be considered resources in and of themselves, including components (individual resources) presented in a specific order with a specific message as the result of an editorial or collection development process, they can also be considered as services providing access to collections. In this vein, the text of a website's home page can be considered a collection-level description. The MARC format allows for the description of a collection as well as individual items. EAD, used for archival resources, also allows for the description of a collection, including its content, context, and organisation. The Dublin Core Metadata Initiative Type Vocabulary includes, among others, the resource types Collection and Service, suggesting that Dublin Core allows the description of individual resources, as well as collections or websites. The suitability of Dublin Core for collection description is further supported by the activities of a Dublin Core Task Group to create an application profile for collection-level descriptions.[16] Collection-level descriptions are used in collection registries[17] such as the Digital Library Federation collection registry,[18] the IMLS digital collections registry,[19] and the enrichUK gateway of digital heritage collections.[20]

Collection-level descriptions are sometimes created for internal purposes, to manage digitisation in a large institution, or simply to manage digital objects once they are created. These descriptions are more rarely used internally for discovery purposes. It is, however, possible to repurpose existing collection-level descriptions to facilitate resource discovery in a different context. When reusing existing collection descriptions for resource discovery, the same care should be taken as for sharing item-level metadata. One should wonder, for example, what do I want users to understand about my collection if the record is displayed in a registry? It can be useful to create a collection-level description for meaningful groups of resources, whether they are tied together by an intentional effort of collection and maintenance, on a specific topic, directed to a specific audience, or linked through a common resource format (e.g., maps). Collection-level descriptions used by registries may be either created by the collection managers in a dedicated form[21] or shared for example in an OAI-PMH data provider. They may also be created by a remote service, based on the information collected on a website and from item-level descriptions.[22] Indeed, some services do not use structured information for collection description at all, but rather rely on information gained from spidering a website. In order to optimise resource discovery in portals, gateways and directories, it is recommended that webmasters create a mission statement on their website homepage as well as a meaningful title for the website or collection that allows users to assess its relevance.[23]

Automatic discovery mechanisms

In order for a service to incorporate a collection of relevant resources, that service must first discover that the collection exists. In some cases, this is performed with human action. The Google webmaster guidelines suggest submitting a URL to Google using a Web form, but also to submit forms to other services such as Yahoo! and the Open Directory project.[24] It is also possible for an institution to advertise a collection of potential interest directly to relevant service providers in the domain. Registries can be used to make sure that service providers know about collections of interest. For example the UIUC OAI registry[25] records all known OAI-PMH compliant repositories and their features. The content of this registry is harvestable, and a great deal of the information associated with the repositories is machine readable.

Other mechanisms exist that allow a web page or a resource to assist a service in discovering new resources. The OpenSearch protocol includes an autodiscovery mechanism in Atom and XHTML/HTML, using a special document type 'application/opensearchdescription+xml'. This document type can then be included in an XHTML tag, for example:

```
<link rel="search" type="application/
opensearchdescription+xml" title="Huddersfield
Uni" href="http://webcat.hud.ac.uk/
OpenSearch.xml">
```

When Internet Explorer 7 and Firefox 2.0 access a page that contains an OpenSearch auto-discovery link, they offer the user the capability of adding that search to the browser search box, therefore promoting access to a resource not previously known.

The HTML LINK tag can be used to discover different versions of a digital resource (e.g., the PDF version of the resource currently displayed in HTML). The unAPI specification[26] uses a similar concept by embedding inside a web pages links to other representations of the same resource. Features such as these allow, for example, a service to discover and choose the most appropriate version of a resource for its context.

This mechanism is not centralised as registries are, but can be used in complement to registry declaration.

Mechanisms to allow the discovery of metadata sources (repositories) as well as of resources (through direct links) are becoming more and more semantically rich, and are enabling an increasingly higher level of automation of discovery. True resource discovery not only implies that the metadata searched and presented is appropriate for a local institution, but also that appropriate information is made available to a variety of services. As seen in this chapter, this includes collection-level information, information on the mechanisms that make the metadata available to services, the publication of relevant web pages and the sharing of reusable metadata that is useful outside of its original environment.

Notes

1. University of Michigan Museum of Zoology. 'Animal diversity web', available at *http://animaldiversity.ummz.umich.edu/*.
2. OAIster (*http://www.oaister.org/*).
3. University of Illinois at Urbana-Champaign. 'Institute of Museum and Library Services – digital collections and content', available at *http://imlsdcc.grainger.uiuc.edu/*.
4. University of Illinois at Urbana-Champaign. 'CIC metadata portal', available at *http://cicharvest.grainger.uiuc.edu/*.
5. Weibel, S. (1996) 'A proposed convention for embedding metadata in HTML', W3C, available at *http://www.w3.org/Search/9605-Indexing-Workshop/ReportOutcomes/S6Group2*.
6. Spinello, R.A. (2002) 'The use and abuse of metatags', *Ethics and Information Technology*, 4(1): 23–30.
7. Perkins, J. (2001) 'A new way of making cultural information resources visible on the Web: museums and the Open Archives Initiative', paper presented at Museum and the Web 2001 Conference. Toronto: Archives & Museum Informatics; available at *http://www.archimuse.com/mw2001/papers/perkins/perkins.html*.
8. Google. 'Webmaster help center – what is a sitemap file and why should I have one?', available at *http://www.google.com/support/webmasters/bin/answer.py?answer=40318*.
9. Source: Google Press Center (2006) 'Major search engines unite to support a common mechanism for website submission: sitemaps protocol will enable Google, Yahoo! and Microsoft to provide more comprehensive and fresh search results', available at *http://www.google.com/press/pressrel/sitemapsorg.html*.
10. Sitemaps.org (*http://www.sitemaps.org/*).

11. Google. 'Webmaster help center – what other formats can I use for a sitemap?', available at *http://www.google.com/support/webmasters/bin/answer.py?answer=34606&query=oai*.

12. See: University of Michigan News Service (2004) 'U-M expands access to hidden electronic resources with OAIster', available at *http://www.umich.edu/news/index.html?Releases/2004/Mar04/r031004*.

13. McCown, F., Liu, X., Nelson, M.L. and Zubair, M. (2006) 'Search engine coverage of the OAI-PMH corpus', *IEEE Internet Computing*, 10(2): 66–73. Available at *http://doi.ieeecomputersociety.org/10.1109/MIC.2006.41*.

14. Battelle, J. (2005) *The Search: How Google and Its Rivals Rewrote the Rules of Business and Transformed Our Culture*. London: Nicholas Brearley.

15. See for example: Broder, A.Z. (2000) 'Identifying and filtering near-duplicate documents', in *Combinatorial Pattern Matching: Proceedings of the 11th Annual Symposium, CPM 2000, Montreal, Canada, 21–23 June 2000*. Hedielberg: Springer Lecture Notes in Computer Science 1848; available at *http://www.springerlink.com/content/ktn21yjul3r379xy*.

16. Shreeves, S.L. and Foulonneau, M. (Dublin Core Metadata Initiative) 'DCMI Collection description application profile task group Wiki', available at *http://dublincore.org/collectionwiki/*.

17. Entlich, R. (2000) 'Is there a good, comprehensive catalog of Web-accessible digitised collections available on the Internet?', *RLG DigiNews*, 4(6): available at *http://www.rlg.org/preserv/diginews/diginews4-6.html*.

18. University of Illinois at Urbana-Champaign. 'Digital Library Federation – digital collections registry', available at *http://dlf.grainger.uiuc.edu/DLFCollectionsRegistry/browse/index.asp*.

19. University of Illinois at Urbana-Champaign. 'Institute of Museum and Library Services – digital collections and content', available at *http://imlsdcc.grainger.uiuc.edu/*.

20. EnrichUK (*http://www.enrichuk.net/*).

21. Shreeves, S.L. and Cole, T.W. (2003) 'Developing a collection registry for IMLS NLG digital collections', in *Proceedings of the International DCMI Metadata Conference and Workshop, 2003 Seattle, Washington, 28 September–2 October 2003*. Dublin, OH: DCMI/OCLC; pp. 241–2.

22. See for example the work undertaken at the National Science Digital Library (*http://nsdl.org/*).

23. On that topic, see for example the handbook by the European Minerva project: Minerva Working Group (2005) *Quality Principles for Cultural Websites*. Rome: Minerva; available at *http://www.minervaeurope.org/publications/qualitycommentary/qualitycommentary050314final.pdf*.

24. Google. 'Webmaster Help Center – webmaster guidelines', available at *http://www.google.com/support/webmasters/bin/answer.py?answer=35769*.

25. University of Illinois at Urbana-Champaign. 'The University of Illinois OAI-PMH data provider registry', available at *http://gita.grainger.uiuc.edu/registry/searchform.asp*.

26. Chudnov, D., Binkley, P., Frumkin, J., Giarlo, M.J., Rylander, M., Singer, R. and Summers, E. (2006) 'Introducing unAPI', *Ariadne*, 48: available at *http://www.ariadne.ac.uk/issue48/chudnov-et-al/*.

10

Technical interoperability

In order to make two systems interoperable, it is necessary to consider the different layers of interoperability as described in Chapter 8: technical, content-related and organisational. Technical interoperability can be enabled using techniques that have arisen over years in a variety of communities. These techniques allow systems to point to and to represent specific types of objects and to eventually transfer them or allow access to them. The technical interoperability layer allows a connection between different systems and promotes communication between them.

Centralised and decentralised search indexes

For search and retrieval of metadata across distributed systems, there currently exist two major methodologies. Data aggregation involves collecting data from distributed repositories ahead of time and indexing them together for user queries. Federated search involves broadcasting a user search to a set of distributed repositories and merging the results for delivery to the user.

Federated search

A federated search across a set of distributed indexes is often called *metasearch*. Each system has its own way of indexing and retrieving resources, best adapted to its content and structure. In the federated search model, as seen in Figure 10.1, all resources reside in local systems from content providers, and the user queries a metasearch portal. This portal then redirects the user query to all target systems. This model

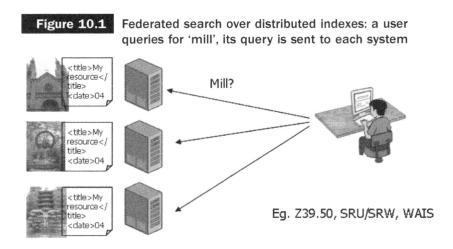

Figure 10.1 Federated search over distributed indexes: a user queries for 'mill', its query is sent to each system

requires that an interoperability layer exists that converts the user query into one that can be understood by each target system. In some cases, this may be a feature offered by the target system, but in others it may be the responsibility of the metasearch portal. Once any necessary query transformation is performed, the new queries are executed simultaneously on all target systems. Each target system sends back to the metasearch system a set of results. The metasearch system then collects these results, and merges them together for delivery to the user. The primary advantage of metasearching over data aggregation is that metasearching ensures data returned by the portal is as fresh as possible; that is, as fresh as in each of the distributed systems.

Metasearch techniques present a number of technical challenges. Systems implementing this method must merge results generated and sorted by different, possibly wildly different, systems. De-duplication of results is difficult because two local systems may contain slightly (or not so slightly) different metadata for the same resource. Pairwise comparison of records from multiple result sets to try to identify potential duplicates can be overwhelmingly resource- and time-consuming. The usage of unique identifiers for resources can help with the identification of duplicates, but this technique is far from universal in practice.

Speed is a second major challenge to the success of metasearch systems. The search is performed in real time, only after a user has initiated a query. The time it takes to send the search to the targets, receive the results, and process them is all time that the user is actively waiting for search results to appear. The design of metasearch systems is therefore extremely sensitive to delays that occur anywhere along the information chain. Due to this time factor, major reprocessing of the data returned by the target systems is generally not feasible. Moreover, the system's performance in time is limited to some extent by the performance of the slowest target system. Some target systems may be out of order or unreachable at the time the query is sent. Others may have a generally slow response time. The metasearch system must wait for the slowest target system before it is able to present any kind of truly merged results to the user. This feature makes metasearch very sensitive to the multiplication of distributed search targets and to the continued growth of their content. Trade-offs between speed and value can be made, such as not de-duplicating results, not merging results, or simply returning search results to the user as they are received from target systems instead of waiting for the whole list of result to present them, as seen in the Copernic Agent.[1]

The final major challenge to metasearch engines is that to work most effectively, each target system must implement a metasearch layer. Without this layer, the metasearch engine must resort to brute-force techniques, such as parsing HTML, that are likely to be unpredictable or unstructured. The implementation of a metasearch layer by each target can be fairly sophisticated. However, it adds value as it makes the resources contained in the target system more accessible, and allows the metasearch system constant access to the newest 'live' versions of data. Metasearch layers also make it easier to implement customised search algorithms, optimised for each target system. To promote interoperability, a metasearch layer might include features such as

- a definition of indexes that can be searched according to a given syntax;

- a definition of one or more metadata profiles used in the results sets.

The Z39.50 protocol, well implemented in the library community, is one example of a metasearch strategy (see also the DiGIR – for Distributed Generic Information Retrieval – protocol, used notably in natural history museums; *http://www.specifysoftware.org/Specify/specify/Specify%20DiGIR/*). Specific profiles have been created for Z39.50 to support the metadata common within a given community. For example, the Z39.50 Bath profile defines indexes and results formats for cross-domain applications in the library, archives and museum communities.

A next-generation, Web-based adaptation of Z39.50 is emerging, called SRU (Search/Retrieve via URL). The default, most used, version of SRU passes query parameters using HTTP GET, however, SRU methods for issuing queries via HTTP POST and SOAP are also supported. SRU uses a specific query language developed together with the SRU protocol: CQL (Common Query Language). Both SRU and CQL are maintained by the Library of Congress.[2] CQL includes context sets that are used in profiles for the definition of search indexes and results sets. Although it is still not widely implemented, SRU has gained a great deal of interest (see Figure 10.2 for an example implementation). It has motivated the creation of advanced services such as D+ (Brokerage for Deep and Distributed e-learning Resources project) at the University of Edinburgh Library[3] and the Metasearch XML Gateway at the Library of Congress.[4] Libraries and other cultural heritage institutions are increasingly facilitating distributed searching of their collections.[5]

Figure 10.2 Interface of the European Library hosted at the Koninklijke Bibliotheek (Netherlands), based on SRU access to the collections listed on the left-hand side of the screen[6]

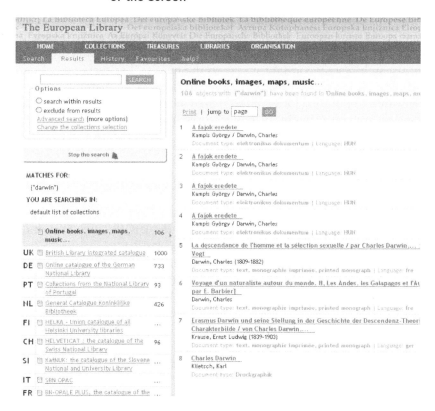

The OpenSearch/A9 protocol is much simpler than Z39.50 and SRU. This protocol was developed in the commercial sector by A9,[7] which powers Amazon's search engine, and not by the cultural heritage community. It uses centralised indexes for simplified keyword-based searches. The protocol supports responses formatted in HTML, in XML or as an RSS feed. The protocol, despite its commercial roots, has been implemented in cultural heritage institutions: for example, at the University of Huddersfield's Library. Huddersfield's OpenSearch target can be queried using the following syntax:

http://webcat.hud.ac.uk:4128/rest/keyword/general/{searchTerms}

Data aggregation

An alternative to federated (just-in-time) searching is the aggregation approach, which relies on a centralised search index against which user queries are submitted (see Figure 10.3). With this method, only the subset of information needed to perform specific functions (most commonly search and retrieval) is shared between a content provider and an aggregator. This subset can include only metadata, or it can also include other views of resources, such as their representations in indexes. This subset of information necessary to drive a third-party service is then collected and stored by that service in a centralised location. This method therefore eliminates the need to centralise the resources themselves.

Figure 10.3 Data aggregation – a central system collects all the information it needs and leaves the resources on their source system

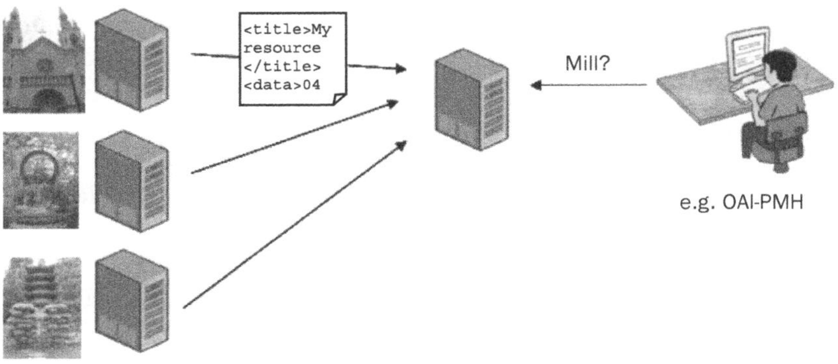

```
<title>My
resource
</title>
<data>04
```

Mill?

e.g. OAI-PMH

For the aggregation method to be effective, a protocol implementing it must address the following critical issues:

- definition of a specification for an aggregator to collect remote data;
- definition or communication of the metadata for representing resources supported by the protocol;
- a mechanism for determining the freshness of the information obtained;
- a method for managing links between metadata records and resources.

Aggregation alleviates some of the challenges of the federated search model. Merging result sets from different systems in real time is not necessary, as only one pre-aggregated index is being searched. Response time from target systems is a less critical issue as the communication between the central system and target systems occurs without the end-user's involvement. As the data is aggregated ahead of time, more intense processing, including data normalisation, can be performed without slowing down the search time for any given end-user.

Aggregation, however, also carries its own challenges. As data is pre-fetched, its freshness can be an issue. Most aggregators revisit content providers to learn of new content or updates on a regular schedule (say, once a month). As a result, the data in the central portal may be obsolete. Edits or corrections made to the data in a local system may take a while to be picked up centrally. For example, if a resource was removed from its original system, then the link to that resource on the portal side will be broken until the central portal visits the local system again. Some services plan for this eventuality by storing the entire resource in a cache. In case a link is broken, the service can display its own version of the resource instead of the version from the originating system. If new resources were added to a content provider, they will not appear in the central portal until the portal service revisits the content provider. For certain types of resources, or for certain use models, the downside of outdated data can outweigh the advantage of having a single access point to search the resources in distributed systems.

The limitations of aggregation can be more problematic for certain types of applications than for others. For example, institutional repositories often have policies for maintaining stable if not persistent URLs to resources and for ensuring that once a resource is submitted to the system, it cannot be removed. As a result, the risk of creating broken links is limited, and users of aggregations of this type of content can be relatively certain that the resources they find will actually be accessible.

However, in institutional repositories, new additions are constant (as opposed to many collections digitisation projects where materials are ingested in bulk). A central portal operating on an aggregation model that visited individual content providers infrequently would therefore be of little use as a service that provides constant updates to the latest research in a given domain.

Web spiders are an early example of the aggregation approach. With this method, a program follows links encoded in web pages or collects URLs from page authors. The Web spider software indexes the page content and records all other information necessary for the search engine. Webmasters can communicate with spiders via a file called robots.txt that specifies, for example, directories or file types that should be excluded from the discovery process.[8] The frequency of updates for indexes varies considerably between search engines. The information recorded by the search engine in index files typically includes a file's textual content, administrative metadata (for example, last update date) and other types of metadata based on links contained in the page, its URL, and so on.

The traditional method of following links to discover new resources has limitations. For example, a Web spider has to visit every single page of a website to know if any of them have changed. The discovery of dynamically generated pages can also be problematic. Instead of declaring every single page to every single search engine, the main search engines have developed protocols for webmasters to communicate the URLs they can index, such as the sitemap protocol described in Chapter 9.

Another commonly-used aggregation method in the cultural heritage sector is the Open Archives Protocol for Metadata Harvesting (OAI-PMH).[9] The OAI-PMH protocol was originally conceived as a minimal interoperability layer between repositories of scholarly publications (ePrints). In ePrints repositories or archives, researchers can self-archive their papers, including versions of papers after they have been published (postprints) or before (preprints). The cultural heritage sector was involved with the testing and refinement of the OAI-PMH protocol at its early stages. The protocol promised a low-level interoperability system that could represent an alternative to metasearch systems. Indeed, the library community in particular had used Z39.50 as a method for bringing together distributed repositories for years and was aware of a number of its limitations, as mentioned earlier in this chapter. Early experiments with OAI-PMH were performed in the museum community as an initiative of the CIMI (Consortium for Interchange of Museum Information).[10] In the library community, a grant from the Mellon foundation funded seven major implementations of the protocol aiming to investigate specific aspects of its application, including many types of data from heritage and academic communities.

OAI-PMH divides the world into two categories of actors. Data providers expose metadata about their resources through the protocol. Service providers harvest the exposed metadata from one or more providers. They then build services, such as search portals, on top of the metadata aggregation, as seen in Figure 10.4. Like other aggregation methods, an OAI-PMH service provider can periodically visit data providers to determine 'what's new' since its last visit: new records, deleted records, and modified records. OAI-PMH defines this update procedure, without the need for re-harvesting all data previously transferred, as an incremental harvest. The service provider uses the updated information to make changes to its central index, copy any needed records, possibly process them,[11] and make them available to end-users.

Figure 10.4 Picture Australia search on OAI-harvested records from multiple institutions[12]

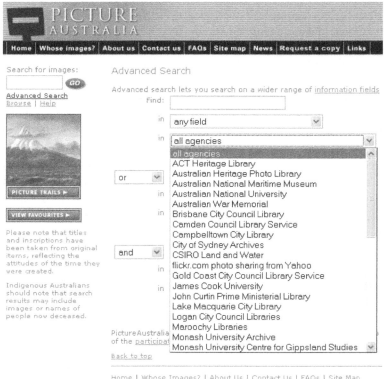

The OAI-PMH protocol defines a series of verbs (see Box 10.1) that must be supported by a data provider to transfer structured information. The protocol uses HTTP to transfer content and XML to format the content that is transferred. An additional requirement is that all items in the repository must be described using an unqualified (simple) Dublin Core record. An OAI-PMH item can be 'expressed' in multiple formats, that is, according to different XML Schemas, but one of those formats

---

Box 10.1   **The OAI-PMH protocol**

The OAI-PMH protocol supports six verbs that allow to collect metadata records from a data provider's repository. In the above example, the repository is located at the following URL: *http://aerialphotos.grainger.uiuc.edu/ oai.asp*. The harvesting takes the form of an HTTP GET request using the OAI verbs and specific parameters.

- Identify: identifies the repository *http://aerialphotos.grainger .uiuc.edu/oai.asp?verb=Identify*

- ListSets: lists the OAI sets defined in the repository and their descriptions *http://aerialphotos.grainger.uiuc .edu/oai.asp? verb= ListSets*

- ListRecords: lists the records of the format defined in the metadataPrefix parameter *http://aerialphotos.grainger.uiuc.edu/ oai.asp?verb=ListRecords&metadataPrefix= oai_dc*

- ListMetadataFormats: lists the metadata formats in which at least one item is available, together with a link to the schema that defines each format and the short name used in the system to define the metadataPrefix parameter *http://aerialphotos.grainger .uiuc.edu/oai.asp?verb=ListMetadataFormats*

- ListIdentifiers: lists the identifiers of all the items represented in the repository *http://aerialphotos.grainger .uiuc.edu/oai.asp? verb=ListIdentifiers&metadataPrefix= oai_dc*

- GetRecord: returns a specific record based on a given metadataPrefix and an item identifier *http://aerialphotos .grainger.uiuc.edu/oai.asp?verb=GetRecord&identifier=oai: aerialphotos.grainger.uiuc.edu:AP-1A-1-1940&metadataPrefix=oai_dc*

must be unqualified Dublin Core. Meta-information is also added to OAI-PMH records: a datestamp of last modification for the record, an identifier for the record (rather than for the resource), describing rights affecting metadata records (again, rather than over the resource), etc. This meta-metadata facilitates the communication between data providers and service providers, and increases the traceability of records.

Related items in an OAI-PMH repository can optionally be grouped together into 'sets'. Sets can be distinct, hierarchical, or overlapping. Sets are defined by the data provider according to whatever criteria make sense, for example, by subject, by collection, by access restrictions, or by what is likely to be of interest to a given service provider. These criteria may very well overlap, resulting in items appearing in multiple sets. A service provider can selectively harvest sets of interest from a data provider instead of the full repository. The protocol however does not allow a service provider to perform a search within data provider system to make its own dynamic selection of interesting material. In this case it is necessary to harvest an entire repository or specific sets, then filter out uninteresting records.

The protocol does not directly address linking issues, that is, how the data harvested can relate to a resource in the original system. OAI-PMH was conceived to convey metadata that could point out to the actual digital resources stored on the data provider's site. The link between the metadata record and the digital resource is usually encoded in a metadata value, but nothing in the protocol specifies any mechanism to make this link identifiable and reliable.

The OAI-PMH designers imagined that knowledge communities would agree on specific profiles for both technical implementations and metadata sharing practices. While this level of organisation has not been the norm for OAI-PMH implementers, some communities have risen to this challenge, including the Open Language Archives Community (OLAC),[13] and under the auspices of the Digital Library Federation and the National Science Digital Library.[14]

Even though the OAI-PMH protocol does not make any assumptions about the nature of the structured data that is conveyed, it has been mostly used for descriptive metadata. However, 'lead users' of the OAI-PMH protocol have implemented the protocol to share other types of information, particularly transaction logs, authority records and digital documents themselves.[15] These experiments showed that the potential for manipulating digital resources through the metadata records conveyed by OAI-PMH was somewhat limited. The need for more advanced resource sharing functionality, including reliable pointers to resources themselves and describing different forms of a resource demonstrated by experiments on overlay journals[16] and heritage picture collections.[17]

As a result, a new protocol is currently under development under the umbrella of the Open Archives Initiative: OAI Object Re-use and Exchange (OAI-ORE; *http://www.openarchives.org/ore/*). This new protocol will build on the current OAI-PMH base and develop specifications adapted to the transfer or addressing of datastreams (digital resources themselves or parts of resources, or groups of resources). This initiative will be experimented with in different environments, with cultural data, scientific publications, and scientific datasets. This next-generation protocol should take interoperability issues one step further, not only relying on metadata for enabling digital library functions, but also on content itself that can be consistently addressed and located.

Syndication is another method by which metadata can be aggregated. It was originally conceived, however, as a news-sharing mechanism. In this format, a website can list its updates as XML formatted information (a 'feed') that is read by an aggregator program. Feeds convey information briefly, generally containing a title, a description, and a link. Two main formats are used for syndication: RSS and Atom.

RSS as an acronym has multiple meanings: Really Simple Syndication, Rich Site Summary, and RDF Site Summary. RSS was born as a successor to the Meta Content Framework created by Guha Ramanathan, and has gone through several successive specifications. RSS 2.0[18] uses XML syntax and contains an extended set of tags, including administrative data on who is providing the information, and how and when it was provided. (See Box 10.2 for a sample RSS feed.) Atom[19] adds a mandatory unique identifier for each entry as well as the possibility of using HTML or XML tags, base64 encoded content, and the inclusion of digital signatures.

To provide syndicated content, a website administrator has only to maintain an up-to-date XML file that contains the desired feed. End-users can install a reader on a personal computer that will aggregate all the feeds available, or use a Web-based service such as Bloglines.[20] Feed aggregation is also integrated into popular Web browsers, such as Internet Explorer 7 and Firefox 2.0.

Many digital library systems, many blogs, and many websites use feeds to alert users that there is new content available. Feeds are 'close-to-real-time' alert systems that convey short information with relevant metadata. They can be used as systems to provide information to end-users as well as to trigger specific processes in machines.

Box 10.2	Extract of a RSS feed from the Library Journal *(http://www.libraryjournal.com/LJInfotech.xml)*

```
<rss version="0.91">
<channel><title>Infotech News</title>
<description>Library Journal Infotech News
Articles</description>
<language>en-us</language>
<link>http://www.libraryjournal.com</link>
<copyright>Copyright 2007 Reed Business
Information. Subject to its Terms of
Use&lt;/A&gt;</copyright>
<pubDate>Thu, 22 Mar 2007 09:40:56
PST</pubDate><item>
<title>SirsiDynx Announces Forthcoming Rome
Platform</title>
<link>http://www.libraryjournal.com/article/
CA6425428.html</link>
<description>SirsiDynix March 14 announced the
fourth-quarter debut of a new platform
tentatively titled Rome, which is based on its
Unicorn technology.</description>
<!-- eLogic Tracking: articleid=CA6425428,
source=Library Journal -->
</item>
[...]
</channel>
</rss>
```

Identifying and locating resources

The mechanisms of data aggregation and federated search use metadata independently from the resource to which it relates. Metadata records can be moved around on the Web with relative ease. But those metadata records rapidly lose value if the link to the resource they describe is lost. By contrast, the resource may need metadata to be adequately interpreted, for example, with a documentary photograph. The identifier and the locator(s) of a resource are important metadata elements to maintain that relationship between metadata and resources.

A repository or digital library system creates an identifier for any resource to which it provides access. A fully-functional identifier must be:

- Unique: the identifier must unambiguously identify a digital object, or a part of a digital object, or a group of digital objects, or even a concept (for example, a name authority record). No two objects in a repository can use the same identifier.

- Addressable: the object must be addressable and/or retrievable using its identifier. It should be possible to construct a direct link to any given object.

- Persistent: the identifier must be persistent, that is independent from the location of the entity. If a picture is moved to a different URL for example, its identifier remains attached to that picture. Any published identifier should from that point on continue to point to the object, no matter where that object may currently be located.

At any given time, most repository managers can assert that all objects in their repository have unique identifiers, i.e., that no identifier represents more than one object in the repository, and that the identifiers assigned are persistent, i.e., that an object once created will always have the same identifier and that identifiers are never reassigned. However, continuing these practices into the indefinite future can be difficult. Institutions, projects, laboratories and so on can be reorganised; a repository can be abandoned or transferred; internal policies can change.

Persistent identifiers

In the scope of distributed services, identifiers must be unique, addressable and persistent, not only inside a given application, but also across repositories. Identifiers are part of a larger architecture that promotes the unique identification and location of resources. Frameworks for persistent identifiers usually rely on an authoritative third party to assign a unique identifier to a digital object. The location of the digital object is distinct from its identifier. Typically, a resolver service is used to map an identifier to the object location. Current frameworks for identifiers include PURL,[21] HANDLE,[22] DOI,[23] ARK,[24] and URN.[25]

DOIs are a specific application of HANDLE system that was developed in the publishing industry. DOI syntax is specified in the ANSI/NISO Z39.84-2005 standard.[26] DOIs are created by one of several authorised registration agencies, with fees determined by the agency.

A central resolver service takes a DOI as input, and resolves that DOI to the current location of the object. When registering a DOI, it is possible to also provide additional metadata about an object, for example including references to related objects. DOIs do not necessarily apply only to publications. The TIB (German National Library of Science and Technology) for example assigns DOIs (and URNs) to research datasets.

URNs (Uniform Resource Names) *identify* resources, while URLs *locate* digital resources. A number of institutions can assign URNs. However, there is no global resolution system for URNs at this time. URNs can be assigned to any type of entity, and particular communities have developed specifications for URNs that apply to particular types of resources. For example, the Object Management Group and the Interoperable Informatics Infrastructure Consortium (I3C) have defined a definition of URNs for biological entities, known as Life Science Identifiers (LSID).[27]

Global identification

Community practices tend to develop for digital resource identification. Identifiers are needed for many types of objects, including non-digital objects. In order to cope with the wide variety of needs for identifiers, some coordination is needed. The info-URI scheme provides some of this coordination, by encompassing different identification practices for a variety of entities.[28] The scheme intentionally casts a wide net: 'Note that we are concerned with 'information assets', not 'digital assets' per se – the information assets may be variously digital, physical or conceptual'.[29] An info-URI can be assigned to a terminology concept, as well as to an author or a digital object. An info-URI namespace must be registered in the registry maintained by OCLC.[30] For example, ArXiv identifiers are recorded with the info:arxiv/namespace, DOIs with the info:doi/ namespace, sequences records in DDBJ/EMBL/GenBank with the info:ddbj-embl-genbank/namespace, National Library of Medicine PubMed identifiers by the info:pmid/namespace, and the Astrophysics Data System bibcodes by the info:bibcode/namespace.

The OCLC Terminology Services project (*http://www.oclc.org/termin ologies/default.htm*) has defined info-URIs for terminology concepts, using the info:kos/namespace for knowledge organisation systems. An identifier can be assigned either to a scheme (including its version) or to a particular concept within that scheme. If this model develops into a production-level service, it will be possible, when recording a term representing a concept that comes from a controlled vocabulary into a metadata record, to connect that term in a machine-readable way, using the concept identifier, to data about the vocabulary itself.

Link resolution

In addition to the resolver services provided by identification mechanisms such as DOIs, other link resolution methods are used to ensure the persistence of shared links. The OpenURL mechanism for digital object location, for example, was developed in the context of scholarly publications.[31] OpenURLs encode bibliographic information for a particular article (known as a ContextObject), either in XML or using a key-value pair. A link resolver, typically in a library, will resolve the OpenURL and direct the request to the appropriate location in its local system, which will often be in a licensed database. The syntax of an OpenURL is as follows:

> *http://myresolver.edu?sid=ebsco:medline&aulast=Moll&auinit=JR &date=2000-11-03&stitle=J%20Biol%20Chem&volume= 275&issue=44&spage=34826*

and

> *http://myresolver.edu?id= doi:10.1074/jbc.M004545200*

OpenURL links can also be used within auto-discovery mechanisms. The CoinS system is one example of this usage, which provides a mechanism for embedding bibliographic citations in XHTML pages,[32] such as:

```
<span class="Z3988" title="ctx_ver=Z39.88-2004&
amp;rft_val_fmt=info%3Aofi%2Ffmt%3Akev%3Amtx%3A
journal&amp;rft.issn=1045-4438"></span>
```

An application with link resolution capabilities can read a 'preferred' pointer to the resource instead of a URL. For example, the Zotero citation manager plug-in for Firefox[33] (see Figure 10.5) can read a CoinS citation from a web page, record the bibliographic citation in a structured format, and re-export that citation according to any citation style.

The browser recognises bibliographic information on the web page and displays an icon. By clicking on that icon, the metadata is imported in the citation management system.

Figure 10.5 Zotero screenshot

Representing compound resources

Resources can be associated with multiple identifiers and pointers, often because there are multiple representations of the resource or because the resource is complex, containing multiple parts. Each version of a resource, and each component of a complex resource, may deserve to be identified and located on its own. In cases where a resource is available in multiple formats, for example, a video in AVI and MPEG formats, multiple metadata records may be required to represent the digital resource in order to fulfil different functions of the system. A specific link may be necessary to represent the resource in context, for example, an image rendered as part of a collection's website, displayed with descriptive metadata. A number of models exist for linking together multiple representations or resources and of connecting parts to a whole.

Conceptual models such as FRBR[34] or the model that underlies the VRA Core metadata element set, distinguish the intellectual creation (the work) from its multiple representations, although these two models define 'work' differently. In the context of scholarly communication, the ePrints Application Profile (or Scholarly Work Application Profile), developed in 2006 under the umbrella of the Joint Information Systems Committee in the UK, describes the entities modelled in ePrints repositories, as illustrated in Figure 10.6. The application profile supports the fundamental activities of these repositories. Researchers or their representatives (for example, librarians) deposit pre-print or post-print versions of scholarly articles to databases. The content of those databases is usually made available for open access on the Internet. Some communities use ePrints repositories as working systems to deposit early versions of their papers to collect comments from peers. These systems may therefore contain successive versions of an article, or offer the article in various formats. The application profile defines a metadata format based on the conceptual model needed to represent the descriptions of the scholarly work and its various copies.

A digital resource may also be composed of multiple digital files. A book can be composed of multiple chapters, each stored in a different file. An article or dissertation may include external objects such as

Figure 10.6 ScholarlyWork or ePrints application profile model based on the FRBR framework[35]

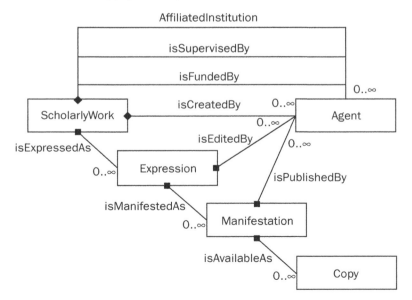

a table or appendices that can be stored in distinct files, even in distinct information systems.

Standard containers have been developed to represent complex resources, composed of multiple representations or parts of resources. The METS XML Schema (Metadata Encoding and Transmission Standard), maintained by the Library of Congress,[36] is perhaps the most heavily used of these container formats in the cultural heritage sector. A METS file can include the set of files that compose the object, structural metadata, descriptive metadata, administrative metadata and behavioural metadata. The METS schema, however, does not define which metadata formats should be used to describe the resource – METS is merely a container, or wrapper, for other types of metadata formats.

Due to the inherent flexibility of METS, in order to effectively share METS files it is necessary to define a profile that describes what can appear in a METS record that conforms to that profile.[37] For example, the METS Navigator[38] application developed at Indiana University displays a multi-page object inside a page-turning interface and provides user-friendly navigation within the object. It uses the structure and the pointers defined in the METS file to access the different parts of the object. The METS Navigator application expects the METS files it reads to conform to a specific METS profile registered with the Library of Congress.[39]

Other standards can be used to embed different types of metadata and resources either by reference (pointers) or by value (the resource itself is included). MPEG21 DIDL (Digital Item Declaration Language)[40] containers, for example, were created mainly for commercial digital objects but are also used in the cultural heritage sector to share representations of journal articles.[41] The IMS content packaging specification defines a container for learning resources also used by cultural heritage institutions.[42]

Current distributed digital library services rarely make use of complex representations of digital resources. Despite human-readable guidelines for representing these complex objects, such as the encoding of identifiers, there is a need for sharing complex objects and multiple representations of digital objects in a more machine-readable form. The Open Archives Initiative Object Reuse and Exchange (OAI-ORE) project, mentioned above, aims to define a framework for representing, addressing and sharing digital resources to promote better resource interoperability. As seen in Figure 10.7, the OAI-ORE framework defines multiple representations of an object, as well as the relationship of parts of objects to one another.

Figure 10.7 A sample (simple) compound digital object as described in the OAI-ORE model[43]

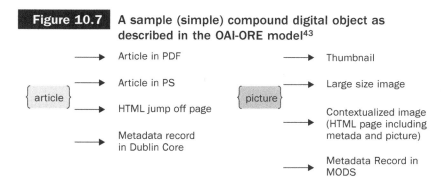

The unambiguous identification and location of resources is key to the development of new types of services. Structural metadata and reliable pointers to different parts of complex digital resources have a major part in certain types of applications. The Asset Actions experiment carried out under the umbrella of the Digital Library Federation demonstrates the utility of this sort of information. The Asset Actions group has defined a format to share pointers for different representations of an object, metadata, and multiple digital formats. The experiment demonstrated a variety of applications that can be enabled when reliable pointers are shared, for example, annotating part of a picture, storing the annotation in a distinct location, and dynamically displaying the annotation on the appropriate part of the resource.[44] A variety of services can be developed from digital resources if a framework exists for the efficient sharing of complex object representations, including metadata and digital resources themselves.

Transforming metadata records

In order to be usable in a new context, metadata must be prepared and potentially transformed from one format into another. For example, the OAI-PMH requires the simple Dublin Core format. The SRU protocol is used with CQL context sets. Original records from the local information system often have to be reprocessed to meet the needs of these sharing protocols. Information may need to be added or removed for a shared record. Some values may have to be modified, perhaps to use a standard terminology. Chapter 11 discusses the preparation of metadata content for sharing purposes in greater depth. Preparing metadata in these ways requires tools and procedures to transform metadata. This process is called *metadata mapping* or *crosswalking*.

Planning for metadata mapping

The process of metadata mapping covers a great deal more than simply converting a record into another equivalent record. The metadata record stored in a local system was created for a specific purpose, to enable a specific set of functions. Metadata elements sometimes depend on each other to make sense. The original metadata format and the target metadata format may differ in the unit of description, in the properties they highlight, and in the encoding of metadata values. These and other factors must be taken into account when performing metadata mapping tasks. Transforming metadata most often entails information loss,[45] moving from a more robust format to a simpler one. Zeng and Chan concur, claiming, 'The major challenge in converting records prepared according to a particular metadata scheme into records based on another schema (...) is how to minimise loss or distortion of data'.[46]

The entity that is described in the metadata record can vary, requiring substantial changes when mapping from one format to another. An EAD record, for example, includes collection-level metadata and potentially more detailed multi-level description. The EAD-encoded finding aid can also be considered as a resource in and of itself. An experiment to generate Dublin Core item-level descriptions from EAD files met with limited success, due to the structure of EAD files, often lacking item-level description.[47] Other approaches have attempted to only map collection-level descriptions from EAD files.[48] The VRA Core model separates data describing the work of art from that describing an *image* of that work. The data from those two separate records must be combined when VRA Core metadata is mapped to a format with a flat structure.

Another primary challenge to effective metadata mapping is ensuring that the metadata in each format describes the expected entity. An element for creation date, for example, will expect a different value if the record refers to the creation of a digitised version of a resource than if it refers to the date the original object was created. Many metadata formats provide strict guidance for separating the description of one version of a resource from another. In the Dublin Core community, this notion is referred to as the *one to one* principle.

The one to one principle, simply put, prescribes that a single entity is described in a single metadata record. For example, a metadata record might describe a physical resource such as a painting. The dimensions listed in that metadata records should be the dimensions of the painting, e.g. 77 cm in height for the *Mona Lisa*. Its creator would then be recorded as Leonardo da Vinci. The digital representation of this object would have different characteristics, for instance it might be a JPEG image with dimensions recorded in pixels. The creator of the digital image would be the photographer and its date would be very recent. The same digital image in another format, for example, a TIFF image, would be described by a different metadata record. The Dublin Core Usage Guide gives this description of the one to one principle: 'In general Dublin Core metadata describes one manifestation or version of a resource, rather than assuming that manifestations stand in for one another. For instance, a jpeg image of the *Mona Lisa* has much in common with the original painting, but it is not the same as the painting. The digital image should be described, most likely with the creator of the digital image included as a Creator or Contributor, rather than just the painter of the original *Mona Lisa*. The relationship between the metadata for the original and the reproduction is part of the metadata description. It assists the user in determining whether he or she need to go to the Louvre for the original, or whether his/her need can be met by a reproduction'.[49]

The one to one principle is difficult to apply in practice, as illustrated by the actual implementation of the Dublin Core metadata set at many institutions.[50] It is, however, important to clarify which entity is represented in each element to adequately map to formats that expect a stricter separation of the description of multiple versions.

Differences in field definitions must be carefully examined in order to perform an effective metadata mapping. A date element in a Dublin Core record may have to be mapped to a more complex format that defines different types of dates. To do this correctly, additional information must be found that identifies what type of date was recorded in the Dublin Core record. Due to this problem, it is preferable to map from a richer metadata format to a simpler one, rather than the other direction. If the concept recorded in a given metadata property is not precise enough in the source format, it can be difficult or impossible to map it automatically to a format that uses two or more distinct elements for that concept. The existence of a metadata creation guide as described in Chapter 3 is crucial to understanding the source metadata in order to perform an effective mapping.

A similar challenge appears when concepts from two metadata formats overlap; that is, when one is not a subset of the other but parts of element definitions mix and match with element definitions in the second format. In this case, it is not clear which part of the element has to be mapped. When performing mappings in this environment, it is important to assess which functions are envisioned in the third party systems that will use the resulting metadata. The same approach as described in Chapter 6 is required: analysing how the data will look in a third party system, among other resources potentially of a totally different nature, and to serve different digital library functions.

When mapping a metadata record to a different format, it is not generally necessary to map all values from the original record. Some values may be left out because there is no equivalent element in the target format, or because their value was assigned for internal purposes. This is the case when mapping to a simpler metadata format or even to a metadata format that has a different perspective on a resource. The technical information related to the digitisation process, such as scanner settings, are extremely important to record for internal purposes and particularly for preservation. However, few external systems need this information to perform their functions, and, in fact, including it may get in the way of the third-party system effectively using the metadata record. In most cases in today's sharing environment, it is therefore better to leave it out. Along these lines, the MARC to Dublin Core mapping proposed by the Library of Congress[51] leaves many MARC fields out of the target Dublin Core record. Table 10.1 illustrates possible mappings between metadata elements in different formats. It clearly shows that in certain formats, there is no logical place for a given piece of information, and therefore it should not be mapped.

In certain cases, two metadata elements in the source format can be assigned to the same metadata element in the target format. Whenever possible (i.e., if the target format allows the repetition of elements), the metadata values should be kept separate. In any further reprocessing of the metadata record, it may be necessary to convert or extract information from that metadata value. This process becomes more difficult if multiple pieces of information are merged in the same field. For example, if a resource has multiple authors, they should be recorded in multiple metadata elements. Otherwise, to display a list of authors, it is necessary to split the metadata values.

Technologies for sharing metadata require that records are flexible. One digital resource in one format associated with one metadata set can be sufficient for local purposes. But to share digital resources, it is necessary to allow a certain level of adaptation and flexibility. In order

Table 10.1 Mapping proposed by the Getty Trust for Object Work (core) in CDWA[52]

CDWA (Categories for the Description of Works of Art)	Object/Work – Catalogue Level (core)
CCO (Cataloging Cultural Objects)	
CWA Lite (XML Schema)	<cdwalite:recordType>
VRA 4.0 XML (XML Schema Visual Resources Association)	<vra: work> or <vra:collection>
MARC (Library of Congress)	655 Genre/Form 300a Physical Description – Extent
MODS (Metadata Object Description Schema, Library of Congress)	<genre> <extent>
Dublin Core	
EAD (Encoded Archival Description)	LEVEL attribute
CIMI (Consortium for the Computer Interchange of Museum Information – Z39.50 profile)	
FDA Guide (Guide to the Description of Architectural Drawings Getty Trust)	Document Classification – Catalogue Level and Group Type

to facilitate that flexibility at a global level, metadata registries[53] have been created to indicate the specific rules according to which metadata formats and application profiles were conceived and the possible crosswalks that can be applied. In order to limit the difficulties in metadata mapping, certain formats such as IEEE LOM or the ePrints/Scholarly Works Application Profile have been written to include a mapping to the simple Dublin Core format.

Mapping tools

Once planned, the actual mapping of metadata can be performed either with a program/script or with an XSLT stylesheet.[54] Mappings can be developed in programming or scripting languages such as Java, Perl or Python.[55] Mapping tools could also be made available through Web services.[56] These services typically take XML files as input and output a new XML file.

XSLT has some limitations in its usage for text processing. However, it has been designed to process XML files, so it is a common choice for implementing metadata mappings. The sample extract from an XSLT stylesheet from Dublin Core to MODS shown in Box 10.3 looks for each occurrence of a dc:relation element in a Dublin Core record. For each of these found, it creates a MODS relatedItem element. It then tests the value of the dc:relation element. If the value starts with the http:// text string, the stylesheet creates a location element, then a URL subelement. Finally, it copies the content of the dc:relation element into the URL element. If the value does not start with http://, the value of dc:relation is copied into a titleInfo/title element in MODS.

Box 10.3   **Extract from the XSLT crosswalk from simple Dublin Core to the MODS format, Version 3.2**

```
<xsl:template match="dc:relation">
    <relatedItem>
        <xsl:choose>
            <xsl:when test="starts-with (text(),
            'http://')">
                <location>
                    <url>
                        <xsl:value-of
                        select="."/>
                    </url>
                </location>
                <identifer type="uri">
                    <xsl:apply-templates/>
                </identifer>
            </xsl:when>
            <xsl:otherwise>
                <titleInfo>
                    <title>
                        <xsl:apply-templates/>
                    </title>
                </titleInfo>
            </xsl:otherwise>
        </xsl:choose>
    </relatedItem>
</xsl:template>
```

Source: XSLT developed by Clay Redding for the Library of Congress (*http://www.loc.gov/ standards/mods/simpleDC2MODS.xsl*).

The number of transformations that can be performed in a single XSLT stylesheet is limited due to practical considerations. For example, if a metadata value in an input document must be split on a semi-colon separator, then each part has to be compared to a set of values and potentially transformed. It can be easier to simply make several stylesheets and process each metadata record with an XML pipeline, that is, a series of XSLT stylesheets applied successively to the metadata record. Each record is loaded in turn, and then transformed. The output of the transformation does not necessarily have to be copied in a file; it can be kept in memory and be used as input for the next transformation.

In practice, certain transformations can be more effective using a programming or scripting language rather than XSLT, typically when a substantial amount of textual processing has to be performed (for example, advanced date processing or subject vocabulary switching), or when one of the metadata formats is not encoded in XML. However, the modular structure of XSLT pipelines, their reusability, and their integration in main XML editors make them very efficient for simple mapping between similar XML formats.

Certain metadata maintenance agencies make available mapping guidelines and even tools such as scripts and XSLT stylesheets to assist with metadata mapping. The Library of Congress makes available mapping guidelines from MARCXML to MODS, Dublin Core, and ONIX. It also makes available a number of additional tools, for example to convert MARC records into MARCXML.[57] Tools to assist with metadata transformation are also available from several websites that collect this information for a variety of metadata formats.[58]

It is important to consider that just as metadata creation has a cost, metadata reprocessing does as well. Customising a transformation streamlined for each collection of the institution or for each distributed collection for a service provider can be very time- and resource-consuming. If the collections grow or change over time, the metadata collection will change and anomalies can eventually appear. These changes can be very difficult to identify, and result in the need for periodic quality control.

The mechanisms that allow the exchange of resources together with their metadata and to address linking together distributed resources or groups of distributed resources are not yet fully standardised. The technological choices an institution makes are dictated by current applications but also by the anticipation of future services that will be built on top of digital collections, either of which might not fit well into actual future capabilities as they develop. Technical interoperability is only one facet of the larger interoperability puzzle: resources, institutional priorities, and planning for the future all affect an institution's ability to move beyond its own walls into the larger networked environment.

Notes

1. Copernic Agent (*http://www.copernic.com*).
2. Library of Congress. 'SRU: Search/Retrieval via URL', available at *http://www.loc.gov/standards/sru/*.
3. JISC. 'd+ Brokerage for deep and distributed e-Learning resources discovery', available at *http://www.jisc.ac.uk/whatwedo/programmes/ elearning_framework/dplus.aspx*.
4. Library of Congress. 'LC Z39.50/SRW/SRU server configuration guidelines', available at *http://www.loc.gov/z3950/lcserver.html*.
5. For more on search protocols, see: McCallum, S.H. (2006) 'A look at new information retrieval protocols: SRU, OpenSearch/A9, CQL, and XQuery', paper presented at the *World Library and Information Congress: 72nd IFLA General Conference and Council, Seoul, Korea, 20–24 August 2006*. Available at *http://www.ifla.org/IV/ifla72/papers/102-McCallum-en.pdf*.
6. The European Library (*http://www.theeuropeanlibrary.org*).
7. OpenSearch.org (*http://www.opensearch.org*).
8. See the robots exclusion protocol 'A standard for robots excusion' by Martijn Koster (1994), available at *http://www.robotstxt.org/wc/ norobots.html*.
9. Open Archives Initiative (*http://www.openarchives.org/*).
10. The consortium no longer exists.
11. See for example: Foulonneau, M. and Cole, T.W. (2005) 'Strategies for reprocessing aggregated metadata', in *Proceedings Series: Lecture Notes in Computer Science*. Heidelberg: Springer-Verlag; pp. 290–301.
12. Picture Australia Advanced Search (*http://www.pictureaustralia.org/ apps/pictureaustralia*).
13. OLAC: Open Language Archives Community (*http://www.language- archives.org/*).
14. Shreeves, S.L., Riley, J. and Milewicz, L. (2006) 'Moving towards shareable metadata', *First Monday*, 11(8): available at *http://firstmonday.org/ issues/issue11_8/shreeves/index.html*.
15. See: Van de Sompel, H., Nelson, M.L., Lagoze, C. and Warner, S. (2004) 'Resource harvesting within the OAI-PMH framework', *D-Lib Magazine*, 10(12): available at *http://www.dlib.org/dlib/december04/vandesompel/ 12vandesompel.html*. See also: Van de Sompel, H., Young, J. and Hickey, T. (2003) 'Using the OAI-PMH ... differently', *D-Lib Magazine*, 9(7/8): doi:10.1045/july2003-young.
16. Van de Sompel, H., Lagoze, C., Bekaert, J., Liu, X., Payette, S. and Warner, S. (2006) 'An interoperable fabric for scholarly value chains', *D-Lib Magazine*, 12(10): available at *http://dx.doi.org/10.1045/october2006-vandesompel*.

17. Chavez, R., Cole, T.W., Dunn, J., Foulonneau, M., Habing, T.H., Parod, W. and Staples, T. (2006) 'DLF-Aquifer asset actions experiment: demonstrating value of actionable URLs', *D-Lib Magazine*, 12(10): available at *http://www.dlib.org/dlib/october06/cole/10cole.html*.

18. Winer, D. (2003) *RSS 2.0 Specification*. Cambridge, MA: Berkman Center for Internet & Society at Harvard Law School; available at *http://cyber.law.harvard.edu/rss/rss.html*.

19. See Internet Engineering Task Force document RFC4287: Nottingham, M. and Sayre, R. (2005) 'The Atom syndication format', *Internet Engineering Task Force*, available at *http://www.ietf.org/rfc/rfc4287*.

20. Bloglines (*http://www.bloglines.com*).

21. OCLC Research. 'PURLs', available at *http://purl.oclc.org/*.

22. Corporation for National Research Initiatives. 'The Handle® system', available at *http://www.handle.net/*.

23. The International DOI® Foundation. 'The DOI system', available at *http://www.doi.org/*.

24. Kunze, J. *Archival Resource Key (ARK)*. Oakland, CA: California Digital Library; available at *http://www.cdlib.org/inside/diglib/ark/*.

25. IETF standard RFC 2141: Moats, R. (1997) 'URN syntax', *Internet Engineering Task Force*, available at *http://www.ietf.org/rfc/rfc2141.txt*.

26. National Information Standards Organization (2005) 'ANSI/NISO Z39.84-2005 – Syntax for the Digital Object Identifier', available at *http://www.niso.org/standards/resources/Z39-84-2005.pdf*.

27. SourceForge. 'LSID Life Science Identifier Resolution project', available at *http://lsid.sourceforge.net/*.

28. IETF RFC 4452: Van de Sompel, H., Hammond, T., Neylon, E. and Weibel, S. (2006) 'The 'info' URI scheme for information assets with identifiers in public namespaces', *Internet Engineering Task Force*, available at *http://www.ietf.org/rfc/rfc4452.txt*.

29. INFO (2006) 'About 'INFO' URIs – frequently asked questions – what was the motivation behind the INFO URI scheme?', available at *http://info-uri.info/registry/docs/misc/faq.html#motivation*.

30. INFO. "info' URI scheme – registry entries', available at *http://info-uri.info/registry/OAIHandler?verb=ListRecords&metadataPrefix=oai_dc*.

31. National Information Standards Organization (2004) 'ANSI/NISO Z39.88-2004 – The OpenURL framework for context-sensitive services', available at *http://www.niso.org/standards/resources/Z39_88_2004.pdf*.

32. Hellman, E. 'OpenURL COinS: a convention to embed bibliographic metadata in HTML', available at *http://ocoins.info/*.

33. Zotero (*http://www.zotero.org/*).

34. International Federation of Library Associations (1998) 'Functional requirements for bibliographic records', in *IFLA Section on Cataloguing*. München: K.G. Saur; available at *http://www.ifla.org/VII/s13/frbr/frbr.pdf*.

35. Allinson, J. and Powell, A. 'Application model', ePrints Application Profile wiki. Bath, UK: UKOLN; available at *http://www.ukoln.ac.uk/repositories/digirep/index/Model*. See also: Allinson, J., Johnston, P. and Powell, A. (2007) 'A Dublin Core application profile for scholarly works', *Ariadne*, 50: available at *http://www.ariadne.ac.uk/issue50/allinson-et-al/*.

36. Library of Congress. 'METS Metadata Encoding and Transmission Standard', available at *http://www.loc.gov/standards/mets/*.

37. Ibid.

38. Indiana University Digital Library Program, METS Navigator (*http://metsnavigator.sourceforge.net/*).

39. Library of Congress. 'METS Metadata Encoding and Transmission Standard – METS profiles', available at *http://www.loc.gov/standards/mets/profiles/00000014.html*.

40. DIDL (ISO/IEC 21000-2:2005 and ISO/IEC 21000-3:2003) is a MPEG21 specification.

41. See: Van de Sompel, H., Nelson, M.L., Lagoze, C. and Warner, S. (2004) 'Resource harvesting within the OAI-PMH framework', *D-Lib Magazine*, 10(12): available at *http://www.dlib.org/dlib/december04/vandesompel/12vandesompel.html*. See also: De Leeuwe, J. and Van Der Velde, M. (2006) 'From repository to eternity: from Delft repository to DARE – the developments of OAI in The Netherlands', *The Journal for the Serials Community*, 19(2):156–60.

42. IMS Global Learning Consortium. 'Content packaging specification', available at *http://www.imsglobal.org/content/packaging/*.

43. Illustration created from the example in Lagoze, C. and Van de Sompel, H. (2007) 'Open Archives Initiative – object reuse and exchange report on the technical committee meeting January 11,12 2007', *Open Archives*, available at *http://www.openarchives.org//ore/documents/OAI-ORE-TC-Meeting-200701.pdf*.

44. Chavez, R., Cole, T.W., Dunn, J., Foulonneau, M., Habing, T.H., Parod, W. and Staples, T. (2006) 'DLF-Aquifer asset actions experiment: demonstrating value of actionable URLs', *D-Lib Magazine*, 12(10): available at *http://www.dlib.org/dlib/october06/cole/10cole.html*.

45. See also NISO white paper: St. Pierre, M. and LaPlant, W.P. Jr, (1998) 'Issues in crosswalking content metadata standards', available at *http://www.niso.org/press/whitepapers/crsswalk.html*.

46. Zeng M.L. and Chan, M.L. (2006) 'Metadata interoperability and standardization – a study of methodology part II – achieving interoperability at the record and repository levels', *D-Lib Magazine*, 12(6): available at *http://www.dlib.org/dlib/june06/zeng/06zeng.html*.

47. Prom, C.J. and Habing, T.G. (2002) 'Using the open archives initiative protocols with EAD', in *JCDL '02: Proceedings of the 2nd ACM/IEEE-CS Joint Conference on Digital Libraries*. Portland, OR: ACM Press; pp. 171–180. Available at *http://doi.acm.org/10.1145/544220.544255*.

48. See AIM25 – Archives in London and the M25 area (*http://www.aim25.ac.uk/*).

49. See the explanation in the Dublin Core usage guide by D.H. (1995) *Using Dublin Core*. Available at *http://dublincore.org/documents/usageguide/*. See also: Shreeves, S.L. (ed) *Best Practices for OAI PMH Data Provider Implementations and Shareable Metadata*. Washington, DC: DLF and NSDL Working Group on OAI PMH Best Practices/Digital Library Federation.

50. The Dublin Core community is developing the concept of 'description sets' to adequately represent the fact that a metadata record refers to multiple entities. See: Powell, A, Nilsson, M., Naeve, A., Johnston, P. and Baker, T. (2007). 'DCMI Abstract Model'. Dublin Core Metadata Initiative; available at *http://dublincore.org/documents/abstract-model/*.

51. Library of Congress Network Development and MARC Standards Office (2001) 'MARC to Dublin Core Crosswalk', availale at *http://www.loc.gov/marc/marc2dc.html*.

52. Gill, T., Gilliland, A.J., Woodley, M.S. and Baca, M. (eds) 'Metadata Standards Crosswalks', in *Introduction to Metadata – Pathways to Digital Information (Online Edition Version 2.1)*. Los Angeles, CA: J. Paul Getty Trust; available at *http://www.getty.edu/research/conducting_research/standards/intrometadata/metadata_element_sets.html*.

53. See for example: Heery, R. and Wagner, H. (2002) 'A metadata registry for the semantic Web', *D-Lib Magazine*, 8(5): available at *http://www.dlib.org/dlib/may02/wagner/05wagner.html*. See also: Hillman, D.H., Sutton, S.A., Phipps, J. and Laundry, R. (2006) 'A metadata registry from vocabularies up: the NSDL registry project', in Dekkers, M. and Feria, L. (eds) *Proceedings of the International Conference on Dublin Core and Metadata Applications – Metadata For Knowledge and Learning*. Colima, Mexico: Universidad de Colima; pp. 65–75.

54. For an example of an XSLT-based workflow, see Foulonneau, M. and Cole, T.W. (2005) 'Strategies for reprocessing aggregated metadata', in *Proceedings Series: Lecture Notes in Computer Science*. Heidelberg: Springer-Verlag; pp. 290–301.

55. Janée, G. and Frew, J. (2005) 'A hybrid declarative/procedural metadata mapping language based on Python', in *Proceedings Series: Lecture Notes in Computer Science*. Heidelberg: Springer-Verlag; pp. 302–13, *http://www.springerlink.com/openurl.asp?genre=article&id=doi:10.1007/11551362_27*.

56. Experiments have been carried out. For example, see: OCLC. 'Metadata schema transformation services', available at *http://www.oclc.org/research/projects/mswitch/1_schematrans.htm*. See also: Emory University Digital Library Research Initiative. 'Metadata Migrator', available at *http://www.metascholar.org/sw/mm/*.

57. Library of Congress Network Development and MARC Standards Office. 'MARCXML – MARC21 XML Schema', available at *http://www.loc.gov/standards/marcxml/*.

58. See for example: Day, M. 'Metadata mapping between metadata formats'. Bath, UK: UKOLN; available at *http://www.ukoln.ac.uk/metadata/interoperability/*.

11

Content interoperability: shareable metadata

Some models for aggregating and using metadata from diverse sources

While technical interoperability is essential for the mechanics of sharing digital objects and their metadata, *content* interoperability directly affects what can be done with those objects and metadata once they have been exchanged. Here, content interoperability refers to the degree to which an aggregator can understand and effectively use descriptive metadata generated by others. According to this point of view, achieving content interoperability is dependent on finding the right balance between the work of the provider of metadata and that of the aggregator, for a specific set of resources, in a defined community.

Simply enforcing a small set of metadata standards that all repositories must use would, on the surface, make content interoperability easier by forcing the metadata records shared to be more predictable and easier to process, thus more easily allowing powerful discovery capabilities on that metadata. Yet even within the somewhat ill-defined scope of 'cultural heritage institutions', this approach is simply not practical. For all the reasons described in Chapter 2, no single metadata structure standard, content standard, or controlled vocabulary is appropriate for use in all cases, and no single set of these standards can realistically be foisted upon all metadata creators in cultural heritage institutions who wish to share their data or metadata. In general, the more consistent data or metadata is, the easier it will be for an aggregator to provide more than simple indexing and discovery, although a variety of methods exist to normalise and enhance diverse sets of data. The challenge, therefore, is to make the best and most appropriate use of the technology and processing power of the aggregator together with the content knowledge of the data or metadata creator. The optimum balance is likely to be different for different types of materials and in different communities. A handful of possible approaches, each employing a different balance between the content provider and the aggregator, are discussed below.

The Google approach

The Google approach, or more generally, that of Web search engines, is the only one discussed here that operates on full content rather than metadata records that serve as surrogates for content. This approach has a number of advantages, including the fact that it can be performed on exceedingly large numbers of documents[1] quickly, and that small improvements to the logic can easily be applied retroactively to documents already processed. This approach faces steep challenges in handling differences in types of content, however; algorithms used to process and understand text for a search engine share little in common with those needed to process a still image, musical audio, speech audio, or video. While Web search engines by no means focus exclusively on text, text is where they began and it is still their greatest strength today. The Google approach puts breadth before depth, focusing on applying some level of processing to more documents. While this approach is remarkably effective, and growing more so every day, the state of the art is still a long way from providing more advanced discovery capabilities desired by some users for some types of materials, for example, by genre of a novel, by date that content (not this specific carrier) was created, or by the name of an individual pictured in a piece of visual media. Furthermore, the state of the art in this area is hidden behind trade secrets in a relatively small number of companies. While cultural heritage institutions are free to use the major Web search engines as inspiration for developing their systems, there is not a body of code or algorithms related to the state of the art that they can easily obtain and re-use for new applications. Google appears to be expanding their approach by experimenting with supplementing its existing processes with more structured (and often human-generated) metadata, under the guises of the Google Books Advanced Search,[2] which, as of July 2007 includes fielded searches for title, author, publisher, publication date, and ISBN; Google Custom Search,[3] which allows users to create specialised Google search boxes, search refinement filters, and specialised search results based on selecting and describing groups of related websites; and Google Image Labeler,[4] a site which matches two individuals online and challenges them to think of the same terms to describe an image shown, providing descriptions of those images to Google.

The CDP approach

The Colorado Digitization Program (later renamed the Collaborative Digitization Program as it expanded beyond Colorado) 'began in the fall of 1998 as the Colorado Digitization Project, funded by a Library Services and Technology Act (LSTA) grant through the Colorado State Library',[5] and was later expanded with the help of a number of other grants. Content for the CDP's various initiatives came from libraries, museums, historical societies, and other cultural heritage institutions with collections relevant to the CDP goal of collecting 'the written and visual record of Colorado's history, culture, government, and industry'.[6] The CDP's basic approach to metadata collection was to publish a set of metadata best practices[7] and expect project participants to ensure the *content* of their contributed records fulfilled the best practices, but to provide tools for each of the participant institutions to actually perform the transformation of records from their local format to the version of qualified Dublin Core that the CDP used as an internal format. Local institutions created custom mappings from local data to the CDP's qualified Dublin Core, and used these mappings to load data in a variety of formats, including MARC and fielded data in Microsoft Access, Microsoft Excel, FileMaker Pro, and delimited text files into the aggregated system through a locally-created tool called DC Builder.[8] The CDP's metadata aggregation activities are generally considered to be a success, although project staff do report that challenges still exist in achieving metadata interoperability through this model, including differences in vocabularies, difficulty in creating crosswalks to CDP Dublin Core, and the inability of some local systems to record all the metadata desired by the CDP's model.[9]

The NSDL approach

The National Science Digital Library (NSDL) project '... was created by the National Science Foundation to provide organised access to high quality resources and tools that support innovations in teaching and learning at all levels of science, technology, engineering, and mathematics education'.[10] The NSDL collection development policy casts a wide net, advising that 'since almost all scientific materials have the potential to be used in some aspect of education, this scope is very broad'.[11] The NSDL's collections include scholarly papers, simple websites, lesson plans, government reports, and bibliographies. The

NSDL team approached this grand mission with an architecture that harvested simple Dublin Core records with OAI-PMH and developed a version of qualified Dublin Core that contributors were encouraged, but not required, to use.[12] The NSDL model is to provide training (including online documentation),[13] but to rely on collection submitters to themselves generate metadata that conforms to NSDL expectations for resources they contribute to the NSDL, and to make this data available via OAI-PMH. Harvested metadata is then subjected to a series of 'safe transforms', automatic processes that 'enhance the information present in the original metadata with no risk of degradation'. Safe transforms fall into three categories: removing noise, identifying controlled vocabularies used, and normalising presentation.[14] This approach is among the easiest technically to set up, although it is far from trivial, and can be expected to scale to large amounts of data reasonably well. However, the NSDL team found both technical and organisational challenges with this approach. Even with these normalisation processes in place, the NSDL staff found that providing robust services on the harvested metadata was a challenge due to quality problems. The project team found that metadata aggregation of resources from multiple environments '... is less effective in a context of widely varied commitment and expertise. Few collections were willing or able to allocate sufficient human resources to provide quality metadata'.[15] They concluded that to provide quality metadata for aggregation, metadata providers needed individuals with each of the following skills: domain expertise, metadata expertise and technical expertise.[16]

The DLF Aquifer approach

The Digital Library Federation's Aquifer initiative was created 'to promote effective use of distributed digital library content for teaching, learning, and research in the area of American culture and life'.[17] Participation in Aquifer is open to members of the Digital Library Federation, and currently 16 libraries have joined. As part of the initiative, Aquifer is harvesting metadata via OAI-PMH for collections from participant libraries and affiliated institutions that fit the subject scope of the project. The Aquifer project has intentionally set its standards for metadata fairly high, especially as compared to the CDP and NSDL projects discussed above. To participate, institutions must expose metadata in the Metadata Object Description Schema (MODS) format via OAI-PMH. In addition, the Aquifer Metadata Working Group has developed a set of best practices[18] to which records harvested for the initiative are encouraged to conform. Aquifer is currently considering policy issues surrounding how closely to the guidelines metadata should conform to be acceptable to the project or to provide higher-level services. This higher-barrier approach, as opposed to those discussed above, is possible due to the fact that Aquifer participants are all academic libraries with staff trained in the areas identified by NSDL as necessary for creating quality metadata. Each institution has also, as a condition of participation in the Aquifer initiative, made a commitment to providing the resources necessary to make their metadata available in the ways the project plan requires. Aquifer is still a young project, however, and it remains to be seen if this commitment is sufficient to build a critical mass of aggregated metadata on the topic of American culture and life.

The OLAC approach

The Open Language Archives Community (OLAC) 'is an international partnership of institutions and individuals who are creating a worldwide virtual library of language resources by ... developing a network of interoperating repositories and services for housing and accessing such resources'.[19] This community has taken advantage of the opportunity for community-specific resource sharing from the beginning offered by OAI-PMH, which from its early days expected specific domains to develop and use their own metadata standards. As Carl Lagoze and Herbert Van de Sompel, the creators of the OAI-PMH protocol, put it, 'The OAI takes the approach of strictly separating simple discovery from community-specific description. Community-specific description, or metadata specificity, is addressed in the technical framework by support for parallel metadata sets'.[20] In other words, metadata providers can *supplement* the baseline simple Dublin Core metadata required by OAI-PMH with additional formats, including those intended for use by a specific community. OLAC has done just this, by developing a metadata standard based on qualified Dublin Core (allowing 'community-specific qualifiers') intended especially for language resources.[21] The most important extensions to Dublin Core made by the OLAC community are an element to distinguish language of the resource from the subject language, extended lists of language codes, and a vocabulary for the linguistic type of a resource.[22]

This approach works for OLAC largely due to its cooperative nature. Support for development of the aggregation of resources came from 'three international linguistic service organisations: the Linguistic Data Consortium (LDC), SIL International, and LINGUIST list'.[23] Two different aggregators taking different approaches to discovery have been created by harvesting data providers making OLAC metadata available.[24] For this close-knit community, a data provider can feel comfortable making a greater effort to conform to community standards, because the aggregations created by the community are among the most valuable tools for research on linguistic materials. The OLAC community continues to thrive, with frequent workshops and new additional data providers being brought online.[25]

The NINES approach

The NINES initiative ('a networked interface for nineteenth-century electronic scholarship'), 'is working to establish an integrated publishing environment for aggregated, peer-reviewed online scholarship centred in nineteenth-century studies, British and American'.[26] One core service of NINES is to provide search access to 'a federation of peer-reviewed resources and innovative research tools', allowing constraints on keyword searches based on genre, year, name, and contributing site.[27] The NINES initiative has not made final decisions about how to collect this content for its production service, nor has it finalised expectations for the format of text or metadata contributed. An initial NINES proposal, however, sets an extremely high bar for contributors to meet in preparing content for inclusion in the federation, including specifying an RDF syntax for metadata and linking to full text, and prescribing a particular genre vocabulary.[28] This approach is likely to be most effective in communities that have a great deal of local technical support, or are made up of motivated and tech-savvy scholars that devote large chunks of time to individual documents, such as literary scholars.

The PCC approach

The Program for Cooperative Cataloging (PCC) 'is an international cooperative effort aimed at expanding access to library collections by providing useful, timely, and cost-effective cataloguing that meets mutually-accepted standards of libraries around the world'.[29] The program is managed by the Library of Congress, and is an umbrella for a suite of programs that support the cooperative cataloguing process. One of these programs, BIBCO, the program for monographic bibliographic records, outlines a set of core MARC record standards that must be used for a MARC record to be coded with the PCC designation.[30] The standards represent a high level of quality as defined by the MARC/AACR cataloguing tradition. Institutions (or groups of them) that join the BIBCO project must complete a training course and contribute a specific number of PCC-coded records to the project per year.

The advantages to the larger community of this relatively strict approach to record creation are many. In an environment where individual published items may be held by potentially hundreds or thousands of libraries, the re-use of cataloguing records among institutions is essential. The PCC program is a mechanism that encourages institutions to spend the time creating higher than minimal-level records, and provides a simple means to identify the record as meeting the core standard for institutions wishing to use the record. The commitment made to the program by PCC institutions, however, is significant. Institutions must invest significant amounts of their own resources to achieve the shared standards, even if the details of those standards don't always meet what are considered to be local user's needs. The program also is only useful to institutions that work in a MARC environment and participate in cooperative cataloguing efforts; far from every institution that might benefit from the robust metadata created. The significant benefits offered by the strictness of the PCC program come with associated significant costs.

The current state of aggregations

As seen in the aggregation examples above, there are many different models for aggregating metadata and content from diverse sources. Each has its own strengths and weaknesses, and each naturally fits better for a different type of community. Cultural heritage institutions currently share metadata heavily through OAI-PMH, as described in the previous chapter. The most common model in place today for aggregations is one where the aggregator pools diverse metadata, perhaps performs some normalisation or enhancement routines on it, then provides discovery services to end-users. Typically in this environment, the aggregator then sends the user back to the home institution for access to the full content and native version of its metadata.

The challenges aggregators face in providing reasonable discovery services on diverse metadata are well documented.[31-33] These challenges have contributed to the dominance of aggregators providing only basic discovery services rather than high-level content interoperability. Each aggregator defines what level of interoperability is sufficient for the services it plans to provide. Evolving protocols for sharing metadata and content, such as SRU and OAI-ORE (described in the previous chapter) are likely to push the state of the art in metadata-based services, allowing more powerful discovery services, and promoting more re-use of content in new environments.

The sheer number of aggregations is unlikely to decrease, even as interoperability of metadata and content becomes easier. Both broad and focused aggregations will almost certainly continue to be necessary, to meet different types of information needs. Aggregations centring around specific types of content and within specific knowledge domains are likely to continue to emerge to meet the unique needs of communities. Interoperability among these aggregations will continue to be essential to avoid building more (albeit bigger) silos of information that can't be re-used or shared.

Creating shareable metadata

One theme that appears in many of the scenarios described above is that contributors to an aggregation are making an effort to prepare metadata specifically for sharing with other institutions. Truly *shareable* metadata has properties that might differ from metadata optimised for local use. In most environments, this means a second *view* of a metadata record would be created for sharing in a specific context, different than the record that drives local search and browse access. What follows are some basic tenets describing the features that make metadata shareable.

Shareable metadata is quality metadata

Quality, as described in Chapter 4, is an essential part of making metadata shareable. Quality dimensions such as completeness, consistency, and ambiguity have demonstrated effects on the services an aggregator can provide.[34] Not all quality metadata is shareable, however.

Shareable metadata promotes search interoperability

Priscilla Caplan, in her book, *Metadata Fundamentals for All Librarians*, describes search interoperability as 'the ability to perform a search over diverse sets of metadata records and obtain meaningful results'.[35] Shareable metadata facilitates the provision of *meaningful* results (largely compensating for the types of discovery problems described above) through the methods discussed later in this chapter.

Shareable metadata is human understandable outside of its local context

Shareable records should be self-explanatory when viewed in the context of a third-party aggregation together with records from other institutions, and not rely on any information provided by a local system to make sense to a human user.

Shareable metadata is useful outside of its local context

A shareable record standing on its own in an aggregation must *do* something for a user: for example, lead them to an online version of a resource that he finds interesting, identify new resources useful for answering his research question, show which institutions hold resources relevant to their information need, and so on.

Shareable metadata preferably is machine processable

While today's environment doesn't *require* that shared metadata be fully machine understandable, taking action to ensure data elements useful for browsing and search limiting, such as types of resources, dates, and languages, are in machine-processable forms assists an aggregator in providing robust discovery services and helps to ensure records from that institution show up when users make use of browsing and limiting features.

These general principles give rise to a number of more specific guidelines for creating shareable metadata. One framework for describing these principles is known as 'The six Cs and lots of Ss of shareable metadata'. These principles are outlined briefly in Box 11.1, and fuller explanations can be found elsewhere.[36,37]

The transformations necessary to create shareable metadata are generally more complex than simply mapping one field to another. Metadata values may also need to be added to share the metadata

Box 11.1   **The six Cs and lots of Ss of shareable metadata**

Content. Shareable records should contain content appropriate for sharing. A shareable record:

- describes the resources at the appropriate granularity;
- includes only data useful for indexing, display, or metadata enhancement;
- indicates which controlled vocabularies are used;
- provides a clear indication of what links point to.

Consistency. No matter what practices are used, using them consistently is essential to make records shareable. Consistent practices are helpful to aggregators so that they might determine which fields to index and display, normalise field values, and develop and apply enhancement logic to large groups of records at once. Each of the following should be predictable for a group of records:

- fields present and absent;
- vocabularies used in a given field;
- syntax encoding schemes used in a given field;
- granularity of indexing.

Coherence. Shared metadata records should be self-explanatory, and should make sense at a glance to relatively naïve observers. Features of shareable metadata records ensuring coherence include:

- values appearing in appropriate elements;
- each instance of an element containing one and only one value;
- high-level indication of the type of resource.

Context. Shareable metadata records ensure all appropriate contextual information necessary to make sense of the resource is included, and that data that is only of local value is excluded.

Box 11.1   The six Cs and lots of Ss of shareable metadata (*cont'd*)

- Types of data to be included:
  - data applying to all objects in a collection;
  - name of the holding or contributing institution.
- Types of data to be excluded:
  - indications of unknown or missing data;
  - presentational markup;
  - artefacts of local practice to overcome system limitations.

Communication. Communication between metadata providers and aggregators can be essential in ensuring shared records are effectively used in an aggregation. Consider sharing with aggregators the following information:

- the format in which the records are stored natively;
- vocabulary and content standards used;
- how often and under what circumstances records are added or updated;
- analytical or supplementary materials;
- provenance of resources.

Conformance to Standards. Shareable metadata records conform to the standards they claim to conform to, allowing automated processing routines to work. These types of standards all come in to play when sharing metadata records:

- metadata structure standards;
- vocabulary and encoding standards;
- descriptive content standards (AACR2, CCO, DACS, etc.);
- technical standards (XML, Character encoding, etc).

record. Default values may have to be assigned to the whole collection: for example, the name of the holding institution or an intellectual property rights statement. The information added is either intended to make explicit information that is implicit in the local context (for example, that a digital image was published on the Web by Stanford University) or to fulfil new functions that are not implemented in the local context. However, certain types of information, such as technical metadata, that are present in a local record but not useful to an aggregator, should be removed for shared records.

Existing values may also have to be transformed. A general subject-heading scheme may need to be mapped to a format expecting separation of topic from genre from geographic place from temporal data, for example. If the use of a term from a hierarchical vocabulary assumes the local system has access to that hierarchy, some of the hierarchy may be appropriate to include in a shared record (for example, to specify that Rome is located in Italy). For certain fields, data may be recorded in the local record as a code. For shared records, depending on their expected use, it may be preferable to add or replace codes with the human readable value. Whenever the target metadata format allows it, the controlled vocabulary used should also be recorded. Sometimes the terminology must also be mapped from one controlled vocabulary to another.[38]

Generally, the mapping process to create shared records should be documented. The procedures used to map metadata records should be preserved, together with their external references (that is, the XML Schemas). This documentation is important to manage metadata locally, but it can also be made available to third parties. The documentation should summarise the choices that were made on which elements were mapped to which elements, which elements were added and which tool was used to perform the mapping.

Creating shareable metadata does take more time and effort than simply sharing local record views. In the current environment, where distribution and re-use of metadata records is rapidly becoming the norm, it is, however, a requirement. The cultural heritage community is continuing to explore the best models for what sorts of normalisation and processing must be done by a metadata provider and what can be done by an aggregator. While aggregators have the processing power to perform various normalisation and enhancement algorithms,[39] metadata providers know the materials themselves and must ensure that knowledge is adequately represented in shared records. As these practices evolve, the properties of shareable metadata will evolve with them. Many digital asset management systems do not yet support creating a different view of a metadata record for sharing. As more metadata is shared, and the challenges to providing robust services on local views of metadata records become more widely known, the need for this feature should become more pressing, and thus simplify the process of creating shareable metadata in the first place.

Notes

1. The term 'documents' here is not intended to imply only textual works; rather it is used in a much more general sense, along the lines of Buckland, M.K. (1997) 'What is a 'document'?', *Journal of the American Society of Information Science*, 48(9): 804–9. Available at *http://www.ischool .berkeley.edu/~buckland/whatdoc.html*.
2. Google Advanced book search (*http://books.google.com/advanced_book_ search*).
3. Google Custom Search (*http://www.google.com/coop/cse/*).
4. Google Image Labeler (*http://images.google.com/imagelabeler/*).
5. Collaborative Digitization Program (*http://www.cdpheritage.org/cdp/ history.cfm*).
6. Bailey-Hainer, B. and Urban, R. (2004) 'The Colorado digitization program: a collaboration success story', *Library Hi Tech*, 22(3): 254–62.
7. The most recent version of this best practices document is available at *http://www.cdpheritage.org/cdp/documents/CDPDCMBP.pdf*.
8. Bailey-Hainer, B. and Urban, R. (2004) 'The Colorado digitization program: a collaboration success story', *Library Hi Tech*, 22(3): 256.
9. Bailey-Hainer, B. and Urban, R. (2004) 'The Colorado digitization program: a collaboration success story', *Library Hi Tech*, 22(3): 261.
10. The National Science Digital Library. 'About NSDL', available at *http://nsdl.org/about/*.
11. The National Science Digital Library. 'NSDL Collection Policy', available at *http://nsdl.org/about/?pager=collection_policy*.
12. Dushay, N. 'National Science Digital Library (NSDL) qualified DC application XML Schema'. Boulder, CO: National Science Digital Library; available at *http://ns.nsdl.org/schemas/nsdl_dc/nsdl_dc_v1.02.xsd*.
13. Dushay, N. and Hillmann, D. 'NSDL metadata primer'. Boulder, CO: National Science Digital Library; available at *http://metamanagement.comm .nsdl.org/outline.html*.
14. Hillmann, D., Dushay, N. and Phipps, J. (2004) 'Improving metadata quality: augmentation and recombination', in *DC-2004: International Conference on Dublin Core and Metadata Applications, Shanghai, China*. Available at *http://metamanagement.comm.nsdl.org/Metadata_Augmentation— DC2004.pdf*.
15. Lagoze, C., Krafft, D., Cornwell, T., Dushay, N., Eckstrom D. and Saylor, J. (2006) 'Metadata aggregation and 'automated digital libraries': a retrospective on the NSDL experience', in *JCDL '06: Proceedings of the 6th ACM/IEEE-CS Joint Conference on Digital Libraries Chapel Hill, NC, USA*. New York: ACM Press; pp. 230–9.
16. Ibid.
17. Digital Library Federation, DLF Aquifer (*http://www.diglib.org/aquifer/*).

18. DLF Aquifer Metadata Working Group (2006) 'Digital Library Federation/ Aquifer Implementation Guidelines for Shareable MODS Records Version 1.0', available at *http://wiki.dlib.indiana.edu/confluence/download/ attachments/28330/DLFMODS_ImplementationGuidelines_Version1.pdf.*

19. OLAC: Open Language Archives Community (*http://www.language- archives.org/*).

20. Lagoze, C. and Van de Sompel, H. (2001) 'The Open Archives Initiative: building a low-barrier interoperability framework', in *JCDL '01: Proceedings of the 1st ACM/IEEE-CS Joint Conference on Digital Libraries, Roanoke, VA.* New York: ACM Press; pp. 54–62. Available at *http://www.cs.cornell.edu/lagoze/papers/oai-jcdl.pdf.*

21. Open Language Archives Community. 'OLAC metadata', available at *http://www.language-archives.org/OLAC/metadata.html.*

22. Bird, S. and Simons, G. (2004) 'Building an Open Language Archives Community on the DC foundation', in Hillmann, D.I. and Westbrooks E.L. (eds) *Metadata in Practice.* Chicago, IL: American Library Association; p. 208.

23. Bird, S. and Simons, G. (2004) 'Building an Open Language Archives Community on the DC foundation', in Hillmann, D.I. and Westbrooks E.L. (eds) *Metadata in Practice.* Chicago, IL: American Library Association; p. 204.

24. Open Language Archives Community. 'Registered Services', available at *http://www.language-archives.org/services.php4.*

25. Open Language Archives Community. 'News', available at *http://www .language-archives.org/news.html.*

26. NINES, a networked infrastructure for nineteenth-century electronic scholarship (*http://www.nines.org/*).

27. NINES Collex (*http://nines.org/collex*).

28. NINES Wiki. 'Submitting RDF', available at *http://faustroll.clas.virginia.edu/ ARPwiki/index.php/Submitting_RDF.*

29. Library of Congress, Program for Cooperative Cataloging. 'About the PCC', available at *http://www.loc.gov/catdir/pcc/2001pcc.html.*

30. Library of Congress. 'Introduction to the Program for Cooperative Cataloging – BIBCO core record standards', available at *http://www.loc .gov/catdir/pcc/bibco/coreintro.html.*

31. Dushay, N. and Hillmann, D.I. (2003) 'Analyzing metadata for effective use and re-use', in *2003 Dublin Core Conference: Supporting Communities of Discourse and Practice – Metadata Research & Applications.* Seattle, WA: Dublin Core.

32. Tennant, R. (2004) 'Metadata's bitter harvest', *Library Journal*, available at *http://www.libraryjournal.com/article/CA434443.html.*

33. Cole, T.W. and Shreeves, S.L. (2004) 'Lessons learned from the Illinois OAI metadata harvesting project', in Hillmann, D.I. and Westbrooks E.L. (eds) *Metadata in Practice.* Chicago, IL: American Library Association; 174–190.

34. Shreeves, S.L., Knutson, E.M., Stvilia, B., Palmer, C.L., Twidale, M.B. and Cole, T.W. (2005) 'Is 'quality' metadata 'shareable' metadata? The implications of local metadata practice on federated collections', in Thompson, H.A. (ed) *Proceedings of the Twelfth National Conference of*

the Association of College and Research Libraries, 7–10 April 2005, Minneapolis, MN. Chicago: Association of College and Research Libraries; pp. 223–37. Available at *http://www.ala.org/ala/acrl/acrlevents/shreeves05.pdf.*

35. Caplan, P. (2003) *Metadata Fundamentals for All Librarians.* Chicago, IL: ALA Editions.

36. Shreeves, S.L., Riley, J. and Milewicz, L. (2006) 'Moving towards shareable metadata', *First Monday,* 11(8): available at *http://www.firstmonday.org/issues/issue11_8/shreeves/index.html.*

37. Shreeves, S.L. (ed) *Best Practices for OAI PMH Data Provider Implementations and Shareable Metadata.* Washington, DC: DLF and NSDL Working Group on OAI PMH Best Practices/Digital Library Federation.

38. Vizine-Goetz, D., Hickey, C., Houghton, A. and Thompson, R. (2004) 'Vocabulary mapping for terminology services', *Journal of Digital Information,* 4(4): available at *http://jodi.ecs.soton.ac.uk/Articles/v04/i04/Vizine-Goetz/.*

39. Tennant, R. (2005) 'Doing data differently', *Library Journal,* available at *http://www.libraryjournal.com/article/CA606393.html.*

Part V
Conclusion

12

The future of metadata

Metadata in some form has been utilised in cultural heritage institutions since their inception. Metadata practices in these institutions were originally conceived for a specific set of functions (as described by Svenonius),[1] which were typically implemented in particular applications, for example, library catalogues. Yet, increasingly, attention is paid to the way in which metadata impacts usability, management and preservation of digital resources. These institutions are using metadata in ways that go beyond the single view of a resource that is provided by the exclusive use of a single metadata format.

Flexibility of metadata is gaining in importance. The expected functions of information applications in cultural heritage institutions change over time. The potential sources for metadata are diversifying, and harvesting metadata from end-users no longer seems a strange idea. Contextual information not previously considered important in many parts of the cultural heritage community is increasingly recognised for its value in explaining and interpreting a resource and guiding its users.

This diversification can be argued as leading to an *increase* rather than a decrease in the sheer volume of structured metadata. More and more pieces of structured information will likely exist for a given resource in the foreseeable future. Each will be related to that resource but each may be provided at different times, by different agents, or for different purposes. A major challenge facing the cultural heritage sector is to find efficient ways of gathering this data together (at least intellectually), to relating it to the same resource, and to use (and re-use) this metadata appropriately for new generations of applications as they emerge.

Automated metadata generation

As described in Chapter 4, automated metadata generation is already gaining a place in digital project workflows, and this trend will likely continue. Certain types of technical metadata are even best generated automatically rather than manually. Descriptive metadata presents a much greater challenge to automation, however.

Systems and algorithms to analyse documents and their structure are under constant development. The DC Dot utility,[2] for example, is a small tool, easy to test, that generates metadata from web pages mostly by suggesting keywords based on an analysis of the text. Tools like this are far from being useful for unattended subject analysis for most needs within the cultural heritage sector, but the state of the art is constantly improving. While automated classification methods were originally developed to work on full documents, recent work has attempted to apply the same principles to metadata records rather than full texts.[3] Automated content analysis for non-textual documents is an area of ongoing research as well, and these methods could potentially be used to generate metadata for storage together with human-generated metadata, or to perform searching on the fly. Research domains for content-based retrieval of still images and recorded music are particularly active.

Some middle ground between automated and manual methods is almost certainly the best choice for most digital library projects in the current environment. It is likely that many of the automated methods we do use will operate as 'supervised' activities, involving a human to make critical decisions, review output at key points, or develop 'training' material to adjust a system to a new type of content. Adopting automated creation methods does not have to require relinquishing control over the metadata creation process, and the use of these methods does not necessarily mean abandoning any core values deeply held by the cultural heritage community, such as the desire to provide effective collocation of like resources. Our challenge as new options for metadata creation evolve is to continually analyse how they can be used as tools to achieve our discovery and management goals for our collections. While our goals are likely to be influenced by new developments, we can still continue to demand metadata that meets our core values, no matter how it is created.

Web 2.0 ideas: participation and mashups

A recent surge in the number of applications and technologies based on the contribution of users has spawned a term to describe the phenomenon: Web 2.0. The value of these applications lies in the strength and breadth of the user community. Systems for user participation generally fall into four categories: recommendation/reviews, tagging, games, and coordinated efforts. All have potential for use in digital library applications.

Recommendation systems operate in two fundamental ways. The first is to solicit textual commentary and/or numeric ratings from users. This could simply be treated as descriptive metadata, its origin tracked, and this information displayed to a user. The second method is to use usage patterns to infer that a user 'recommends' a resource. This approach is taken in a wide variety of applications, from Google's PageRank algorithm to Amazon's 'other customers who bought x also bought y' feature. Options for ranking or generating recommendations based on circulation data have been analysed or implemented by North Carolina State University[4] and the California Digital Library. The latter concluded from a user study that circulation data as a source for recommendations is useful in only a limited fashion. 'The preferred sources of recommendations cited by participants are faculty, bibliographies and footnotes'.[5] Analysis of which search results or browse options are used most often could also be a source of data for driving recommendation systems in digital libraries.

Tagging systems have emerged as online resources that allow users to manage items of interest to them, for example personal photos in the case of Flickr,[6] or Web bookmarks in the case of del.ic.io.us.[7] The *folksonomy* (the full set of terms applied by users to all objects in a given repository) that emerges from these activities is useful for study as well; it represents the vocabulary actual users use to describe resources. This vocabulary is often markedly different from the terminologies employed by controlled vocabularies in the cultural heritage sector. In the digital library realm, tagging systems could be of use both to solicit description from end-users (which could supplement or in some cases replace structured subject analysis) and as a source of new vocabulary terms. Experiments with tagging are happening in the cultural heritage sector, including PennTags[8] at the University of Pennsylvania, which allows users to tag catalogue records together with Web resources; Steve, a research project from the museum community studying user tagging behaviour for art museum resources;[9-11] and at the State Library of Victoria in Australia which invites users to 'share what you know about this image'[12] (see Figure 12.1). The cultural heritage sector could also look to partnerships with commercial entities implementing tagging systems for cultural heritage resources, such as LibraryThing.[13]

Figure 12.1 Picture displayed by the State Library of Victoria (Australia) – note the link to 'share what you know about this image'.

Tagging systems do not necessarily use completely unstructured data. Flickr has implemented a feature called 'machine tags' as part of a programming interface to Flickr content. Machine tags allow a user to place a tag in a particular namespace, i.e., put it in a particular category, such as 'medium:paint=oil'.[14] The del.icio.us system has added 'tag descriptions' to its service, allowing users to create titles and descriptions for tags used, that other users can view to more fully understand the meaning of a tag. If they prove to be user-friendly, structured tagging systems could be leveraged in digital library applications to more fully integrate metadata created by end-users with that created by specialised staff.

While most tagging systems operate by offering the user an easy way to perform some sort of resource management task he presumably already has a need for, other tagging systems use the concept of fun to entice users to tag, then use the user-created metadata to improve retrieval for a set of materials. Tagging games generally operate on the model of pairing two users and challenging them to use the same tag to describe a resource, or some variation of that model. Implementations of these games exist for still images, such as the ESP game[15] and the Google Image Labeler,[16] and for sound recordings, such as MajorMiner[17] and the Listen Game.[18] A particularly interesting variant on using users to create or enhance metadata is the reCAPTCHA service, which provides distorted text used to fight Web form spam while simultaneously collecting the correct text from an image that has been inaccurately interpreted by an OCR program.[19]

Large-scale collaborative efforts for metadata creation also exist. Wikipedia is likely the most well known, but several appear in the cultural heritage sector as well. In the archival community, users have been asked to contribute to the correction of OCR performed on manuscript documents, using an annotation platform.[20] Project Gutenberg is a long-standing cooperative project that operates on a distributed proofreading philosophy – asking any and all volunteers to proofread as small or large amount of text as they like. The current project evolved from an information sharing initiative begun in 1971, and the Project Gutenberg site today provides access to more than 20,000 electronic texts.[21]

User participation in creating digital resources doesn't have to stop with metadata creation. Both the Web 2.0 world driving user expectations and the increasing capabilities of distributed digital libraries are enabling the re-use of digital content in new and unanticipated environments. It is likely that the division between resources held by a cultural heritage institution and those owned by our users will continue to fade. This division has long been problematic in academic libraries, for example, where professors teach with both library resources and their own, but have traditionally needed to manage those resources in two different ways. Current sharing technologies are making this user-centred (rather than institution-centred) grouping of resources easier. The National Library of Australia's Picture Australia portal, for example, federates picture collections from libraries, archives and museums in Australia. They have gone a step further, however, and asked users to contribute their own digital images of Australia. Contribution by users is done not by asking them to visit a particular site or to go through a lengthy donation process, but rather in an environment in which they likely already operate: Flickr. On Flickr, a 'group' exists for PictureAustralia, and a user simply has to add the tag for that group. By adding a few simple extra pieces of data that would likely be provided by many users regardless, the image can be submitted for consideration for formal acquisition by the PictureAustralia collection.[22]

As part of the project Naming,[23] the community of an Inuit village was asked to help the work of curators in illustrating scenes and pictures of the Inuit community history. Without the output of this project, no trace would be left of the people and events of this place in the past, beyond oral history and human memory. Although not online, this experience illustrates how it is possible to request the contribution of those who are not information specialists to build a community around an archive of digital resources. Another example is the Kete archive in New Zealand,[24] which was created with the contribution of local associations to generate content from the community and illustrate the community memory.

The trend of many academic libraries towards setting up institutional repositories, which contain the cultural and scientific output of research institutions, is geared towards obtaining both digital content and metadata from users. These users are a carefully controlled bunch, however, defined as scholars who have established authority and credibility. These same researchers may also contribute their work to domain-specific portals such as arXiv.[25] The resources deposited in these repositories are not necessarily published and validated material, representing in many cases a category of material that research libraries have not previously collected. Researchers are often expected to deposit the articles themselves, although at some institutions librarians provide support for this activity. Because the metadata in this case is generally created by content specialists who are nonetheless novice metadata creators, it is necessary to provide user-friendly interfaces that allow researchers to quickly deposit their papers. The use of complex controlled vocabularies in systems such as this can be particularly problematic. Institutional repository applications must be designed with these realities in mind, providing metadata creation forms that are as short as possible, importing metadata from other applications whenever possible, capturing as much information as possible from the content itself, and so on.

To facilitate expanded use of digital content, in addition to participating in protocols such as OAI-PMH and soon OAI-ORE, cultural heritage institutions are increasingly looking to content sharing sites as means of reaching more users. Content sharing sites such as YouTube,[26] for example, provide mechanisms for embedding a resource (a video in their case) in a web page, either by the institution or by a user (see Box 12.1). This provides an easy way to allow third party sites, such as blogs, to cite digital objects.[27]

| Box 12.1 | Example of a YouTube link to embed content in third party pages |

```
<object width="425" height="350"><param
name="movie"
value="http://www.youtube.com/v/tRpxKHlRQUc">
</param><param name="wmode"
value="transparent"></param><embed
src="http://www.youtube.com/v/tRpxKHlRQUc"
type="application/x-shockwave-flash"
wmode="transparent" width="425"
height="350"></embed></object>
```

Great benefit can be obtained from integrating user-contributed content and metadata into digital library systems. In order to embrace this benefit, applications and management strategies for digital resources must be expanded to take into account less structured as well as a wider range of metadata types and formats, while still providing high-quality services. User contributions can be part of an institution's metadata management strategy.

Defining a strategy for metadata management

To meet the expanding need for robust metadata services, cultural heritage institutions must define a clear strategy for metadata management. This strategy should include adequate high-level descriptions of the various collections of content handled by the institution. It should identify the metadata that is needed about the acquisition process, the deposit process, the digitisation process, and all other processes that are part of the workflow for digital collections. The strategy should define the necessary metadata to manage the resource and to connect metadata with a series of services. As a result, the metadata management policy reflects the mission of the institution and the collections it holds. When institutional missions evolve, new tools are created, or new collections are obtained, an existing metadata management strategy should allow easier adaptation for these changes.

A sustainable metadata management strategy will also include a component devoted to metadata sharing. A metadata sharing strategy will outline the types of services in which the digital resources should be visible and how this visibility should be optimised to best serve the target audience. Collaborations in joint projects can be a good way of developing a sharing strategy. For example, the CIC Metadata Portal was a project jointly funded by Midwestern Universities of the CIC academic consortium.[28] Some Universities in the consortium already had OAI-PMH repositories, and most of them had previously shared their content previously through Z39.50 gateways and other initiatives, but few had formal strategies for how they would share their content and under what circumstances. Over the course of the project, many aspects of the OAI-PMH-based metadata sharing process were investigated. All of the participating Universities had implemented an OAI-PMH data provider by the end of the project. Each learned a little about how to better share their content. In addition, several of the participating Universities had implemented additional local services, providing guidance to other institutions, leading local networks, and developing their own services, for example, Wisconsin Heritage Online.[29]

When developing a metadata sharing strategy, many questions must be asked. How do I want my content to be viewed by other applications? How will this serve my objectives and my mission? How will I serve my existing audience? How will I look for new audiences? The metadata sharing strategy should include metadata design for resource discovery, but also the development of collection-level descriptions and the implementation of reliable identifiers and location mechanisms for digital resources.

It is also important to state any potential limitations that might be placed on the use of metadata records. While unrestricted sharing of metadata records best promotes the types of imaginative re-use described here, very real situations sometimes intervene and require the placement of restrictions on use. Be careful applying usage restrictions to metadata records; rarely does the loss of control that comes along with metadata sharing override the benefits to the institution of a looser usage model.

Providing the most liberal usage conditions for both metadata records and for content as possible promotes flexibility in the future use of these materials. New and revolutionary usage models are difficult to anticipate, and the effects of any restrictions given may be unnecessarily limiting. The Scientific Commons initiative, which proposes to assign machine-readable intellectual property rights to scientific digital objects, illustrates this principle by suggesting that rights be assigned such that agents would be 'legally allowed to use the next killer technologies at will'.[30]

Evolving institutional missions

Cultural heritage institutions are now heavily involved in the development of new services that often borrow technologies and practices from commercial applications. The evolution of these systems to provide ever better access to digital resources has expanded the missions of cultural heritage institutions. Metadata competencies are increasingly part of these missions. Dedicated metadata librarians have existed in cultural heritage institutions at least as far back as 1995.[31] This particular position, like many others, came into being as a diversification of a traditional cataloguing job. Since this time, many more metadata specialist positions have been created in cultural heritage institutions, with a wide variety of responsibilities.

Cooperation among institutions is also finding its way into mission statements. To support the increase of the creation and exchange of metadata within the cultural heritage community, useful tools are being developed to edit and transform metadata, for example the RDF tools from Simile,[32] free software packages for creating and manipulating MARC data such as MarcEdit,[33] utilities to edit embedded XML and ID3 metadata,[34] and higher-level tools for metadata management systems such as those from OCKHAM.[35]

Evolving sets of tools, competencies, and expertise are developing in cultural heritage institutions. Whereas it would be inappropriate to consider metadata as a *new* issue facing the cultural heritage sector, the continuing changes in information technology requires ongoing evolution of institutional missions. New types of services are often better built collaboratively rather than at individual institutions, and the role of the commercial sector in these developments can no longer be discounted. Including these services in institutional missions is increasingly important. Developing mission statements that cover the creation and distribution of digital content requires in-depth analysis of the way these institutions work and represent their content. This requires definition of the audiences and usage models that will be supported, with room for incorporating new models that have not been anticipated. Metadata models must change in response to changes in usage models. The purpose of a metadata manager in these institutions should be to oversee this evolution.

As demonstrated over the course of this book, all metadata is created in light of a specific purpose, intentionally defined or not. The cultural heritage institutions that are most effective in creating flexible, shareable, quality metadata will be those that explicitly tie metadata planning and creation practices directly into institutional missions that reflect the current environment, and can react to new developments. Only by positioning ourselves to fully participate in the information environment in which our users operate can cultural heritage institutions continue to fulfil our primary missions.

Notes

1. Svenonius, E. (2000) *The Intellectual Foundation of Information Organization*. Cambridge, MA: MIT Press; Chapter 2.
2. UKOLN. 'DCdot – Dublin Core metadata editor', available at *http://www .ukoln.ac.uk/metadata/dcdot/*.
3. Newman, D., Hagedorn, K., Chemudugunta, C. and Smyth, P. (2007) 'Subject metadata enrichment using statistical topic models', paper presented at the JCDL'07 Conference, Vancouver, Canada.
4. Antelman, K., Lynema, E. and Pace, A.K. (2006) 'Toward a 21st century library catalog', *Information Technology and Libraries*, 25(3): 128–39. Available at *http://www.lib.ncsu.edu/staff/kaantelm/antelman_lynema_pace.pdf*.
5. Whitney, C. and Schiff, L. (2006) 'The Melvyl Recommender Project developing library recommendation services', *D-Lib Magazine*, 12(12): available at *http://www.dlib.org/dlib/december06/whitney/12whitney.html*.
6. Flickr (*http://www.flickr.com/*).
7. Del.icio.us (*http://del.icio.us/*).
8. University of Pennsylvania, PennTags (*http://tags.library.upenn.edu/*).
9. Steve – The art Museum Social Tagging Project (*http://www.steve.museum/*).
10. Trant, J. (2006) 'Social classification and folksonomy in art museums: early data from the steve.museum tagger prototype', paper presented at the ASIST-CR Social Classification Workshop, 4 November 2006. Available at *http://www.archimuse.com/papers/asist-CR-steve-0611.pdf*.
11. Chun, S., Cherry, R., Hiwiller, D., Trant, J. and Wyman, B. (2006) 'steve.museum: an ongoing experiment in social tagging, folksonomy, and museums', paper presented at the Museums and the Web 2006 Conference. Available at *http://www.archimuse.com/mw2006/papers/wyman/wyman.html*.
12. See an example on the State Library of Victoria website: *http://www.slv.vic .gov.au/platebk/0/0/0/doc/pb000755.shtml*.
13. LibraryThing (*http://www.librarything.com/*).
14. Flickr. 'Flickr API/discuss', available at *http://www.flickr.com/groups/api/ discuss/72157594497877875/*.
15. Carnegie Mellon University. 'The ESP game', available at *http://www .espgame.org/*.
16. Google Image Labeler (*http://images.google.com/imagelabeler/*).
17. Major Miner – Music Labelling Game (*http://game.majorminer.com/*).
18. University of California at San Diego Computer Audition Laboratory. 'Listen game', available at *http://www.listengame.org/*.
19. Carnegie Mellon University. 'Recaptcha', available at *http://recaptcha.net/*.

20. Couasnon, B., Camillerapp, J. and Leplumey, I. (2004) 'Making handwritten archives documents accessible to public with a generic system of document image analysis', paper presented at the First International Workshop on Document Image Analysis for Libraries DIAL'04, available at *http://doi.ieeecomputersociety.org/10.1109/DIAL.2004.1263255*.

21. Project Gutenberg (*http://www.gutenberg.org/*).

22. Picture Australia. 'PictureAustralia and Yahoo! invite you to contribute your photographs to PictureAustralia, using Yahoo!'s online image repository, Flickr', available at *http://www.pictureaustralia.org/Flickr.html*.

23. Library and Archives Canada, 'Project naming', available at *http://www.collectionscanada.ca/inuit/*.

24. *http://blog.kete.net.nz/*. See also Krajewski, P. (2006) 'La Culture au risque du 'Web 2.0': analyse à partir de la création d'une archive numérique communautaire open source néo-zélandaise, KETE', Dissertation DCB Ecole National Supérieure des Sciences de l'Information et des Bibliothèques, available at *http://halshs.archives-ouvertes.fr/halshs-00120016*.

25. Cornell University Library. 'arXiv.org', available at *http://www.arxiv.org/*.

26. YouTube (*http://www.youtube.com/*).

27. Google Books has implemented a similar mechanism to cite book paragraphs based on widgets. Tungare, M. (2007) 'Share and enjoy', *Inside Book Search* blog, Google: 6 September. Available at *http://booksearch.blogspot.com/2007/08/share-and-enjoy.html*.

28. University of Illinois at Urbana-Champaign. 'CIC metadata portal', available at *http://cicharvest.grainger.uiuc.edu/*.

29. University of Wisconsin-Milwaukee. 'Wisconsin heritage online', available at *http://www.wisconsinheritage.org*.

30. Wilbanks, J. (2007) 'Science commons – copyrights and experiences harvesting open content', presentation at the OAI5 conference, CERN, Switzerland, 20 April 2007.

31. McClellan, G. (1995) 'Job Posting: Metadata Specialist', *AUTOCAT: Library cataloging and authorities discussion group* (AUTOCAT@UBVM. CC.BUFFALO.EDU), 30 November 1995, 14:30:56–0600.

32. MIT Libraries. 'Semantic interoperability of metadata and information in unlike environments', available at *http://simile.mit.edu/*.

33. Oregon State University. 'MarcEdit', available at *http://oregonstate.edu/~reeset/marcedit/html/about.html*.

34. OptimaSC (*http://www.optimasc.com/products/dex/index.html*).

35. OCKHAM. 'Downloads/Services', available at *http://www.ockham.org/services.php*.

Index